TENDING the ˹ ˺

MENDING the

# TENDING the EARTH, MENDING the SPIRIT

## The Healing Gifts of Gardening

CONNIE GOLDMAN

RICHARD MAHLER

**HAZELDEN**®

INFORMATION & EDUCATIONAL SERVICES

Hazelden
Center City, Minnesota 55012-0176

1-800-328-0094
1-651-213-4590 (Fax)
www.hazelden.org

Library of Congress Cataloging-in-Publication Data
Goldman, Connie.
        Tending the earth, mending the spirit : the healing gifts
    of gardening / Connie Goldman and Richard Mahler.
        p. cm.
        ISBN: 1-56838-362-2
        1. Gardening—Religious aspects. 2. Gardens—Religious
    aspects. 3. Spiritual life. I. Mahler, Richard. II. Title.
    BL629.5.G37 G65 2000
    635'.01—dc21

                                                        99-055539

04 03 02 01 00    6 5 4 3 2

Cover design by David Spohn
Interior design by Nora Koch / Gravel Pit Publications
Typesetting by Nora Koch / Gravel Pit Publications

For my mother, Bess, whose love of flowers and plants led me to discover the place where nature and the sacred meet.

C. G.


For my mother, Mary, who taught me how to nurture—and be nurtured by—a garden.

R. M.

We give away our thanks
to the earth,
which gives us our home.
We give away our thanks
to the rivers and lakes and oceans,
which give away their water.
We give away our thanks
to the trees,
which give away fruit and nuts.
We give away our thanks
to the wind,
which brings rain to water the plants.
We give away our thanks
to the sun,
which gives away warmth and light.
All beings on earth—the trees, the
animals, the wind and the rivers—
give away to one another—
So all is in balance.
We give away our promise to begin
to learn
how to stay in balance—
with all the earth.

A Native American prayer

# CONTENTS

## ACKNOWLEDGMENTS

There are many people to thank for their help in writing this book, but I particularly wish to express my appreciation to the many gardeners and garden-lovers who shared their inspiring stories with me. Even though there are too many of these individuals to acknowledge here by name, I feel privileged to have discovered the depth, richness, and texture of their experiences. I also wish to extend special gratitude to my coauthor, Richard Mahler; my Hazelden editor, Stephen Lehman; my Hazelden copy editor, Kathryn Kjorlien; and my literary agent, Gareth Esersky.

Connie Goldman

# INTRODUCTION

In the following pages, you'll find nothing about the practical, how-to aspects of gardening. I've left that to experts with botanical knowledge and horticulture degrees. Instead, I'm going to dig into something much deeper and more personal. My interest is in the *why* of gardening, not the *how*. Keep reading and share my discovery of the passionate feelings and profound insights of those who love, appreciate, and tend gardens. You may be surprised by how many aspects of our daily lives—including our psychological and spiritual wellbeing—are nurtured by time spent in a garden.

Many fine books offer basic, down-to-earth gardening advice. If you want to know the best way to fertilize your annuals or how to control your insect pests, there are books out there that can answer such questions. If you're like me, you turn to these kinds of detailed reference works for critical information on how to keep your plants healthy, green, and blooming. I love to look at volumes that are full of gorgeous photographs of garden plants and can think of few greater pleasures than perusing a seed catalog on a chilly midwinter day.

While such publications are important and even inspiring, they rarely (if ever) discuss what might be called the *spiritual connection* in gardening. That's what this book is all about.

Many of us find comfort, peace, inspiration, and solitude in a garden. We celebrate gardens as places to refresh and revitalize our spirits, to reconnect ourselves with the natural world—and with the forces responsible for nature's cycles of creation and renewal. In the garden, we encounter joy, delight, and the many daily miracles of nature.

I've interviewed many individuals who've said they feel closer to *God*—however you wish to define that term—in a garden than anywhere else on Earth. Many have shared with me their experiences of how the activity of gardening is similar to the rituals of meditation, of reflection, or of prayer. Some have told me stories of how gardens expand their awareness of the inevitable seasons of life and the natural stages of growth and change in the human experience: from birth, through adolescence and maturity, to death.

I am fascinated by the rich inner world of the gardener and by the enduring wisdom and deep spiritual growth that we can derive through our experience of gardens. That's why this book is about finding and celebrating the sacred and the spiritual in a garden, no matter how small or simple, how large or extravagant a particular garden happens to be.

There's no question that what is sacred and miraculous in the garden can inform and illuminate our entire being. The lessons of nature are the truths of the life force that also infuse us with heightened energy, awareness, and creativity.

Since humans are an intrinsic part of the natural world, gardening can help us transcend the sense of separateness we feel toward the plants, animals, and elements to which we are inextricably linked. I'm also convinced that one of the best ways to learn the world's spiritual truths is firsthand, by actively *tending* or physically *being* in a garden. Like most things in life, direct experience is the most effective teacher.

The life lessons and perceptions offered by gardens and gardeners provide the essence of this book. I've learned that visiting or cultivating a beautiful garden often stirs deep feelings that sometimes are difficult to express in conversation. The landscape of emotion doesn't always intersect with the verbal domain. My challenge has been to bring words to the printed page that are powerful and precise enough to accurately describe the healing and restorative gifts of gardens and gardening.

I must tell you, this task has not been easy. After all, feelings are feelings, and words are words. My friend, author Mark Gerzon, has said that trying to describe nature—and our internal response to it—is "like trying to catch a butterfly with a pair of pliers: not only will you look silly trying, but even if you are 'successful,' you will disfigure your subject."

While there is truth in Mark's statement, I know from repeated experience that words *can* touch the heart and feed the soul. Words can convey deep and cherished feelings that clarify values and dictate action.

My partner in this writing venture is Richard Mahler, a longtime colleague with whom I previously collaborated on writing *Secrets of Becoming a Late Bloomer: Extraordinary Ordinary People on the Art of Staying Creative, Alive, and Aware in Midlife and Beyond.* Richard is a passionate gardener who shares my sincere belief that gardens can change lives—and maybe our world—for the better. When it comes to gardening, we share sensibilities and values. While this book is written from my point of view for the sake of simplicity, a *we* could easily be substituted wherever you see an *I.*

Our book is being published at a time of unprecedented inner growth among Americans of all walks of life. Through workshops, seminars, classes, audiotapes, videos, books, churches, synagogues, and discussion groups, we are turning as never before to spirituality and religion for comfort and guidance. This activity represents an important shift in consciousness for Western civilization, which has long relied on technology and rational thinking as a means of problem solving.

This book represents part of the shift from technological to spiritual. It puts forward the belief that gardens are an important metaphor for the essential lessons that must be learned if we are to lead full and authentic lives. It is in the garden that we encounter the creative energies and rhythms of the eternal life force, which both bonds us to everything in nature and fully animates the human spirit. It is this circle of connectedness that is explored and celebrated in the pages that follow.

The miracles of nature and the wonders of our planet are all around us. Our daily lives are filled with their enduring gifts and offer limitless possibilities for self-renewal. I hope that the words that follow, the words of those who love and tend gardens, will aid and enrich your quest for personal growth and spiritual wisdom.

May your harvest be abundant!

# CHAPTER ONE

# The Soul of the Gardener

As we tend our garden, we nourish our soul.

—Anonymous

I'm not sure why, but when I'm in a garden, I feel different. Let me be specific: I feel good. There's something about being around plants—particularly those that are lovingly cared for—that instantly fills me with serenity and joy. When I close my eyes and breathe the heady scent of flowers or hear the gentle rustle of leaves, I'm in heaven. When I get down close to the earth and feel the soil with my hands, there's a sense of connectedness to the living universe that opens my heart as nothing else can.

Perhaps my feelings are stirred by a primal urge dictated by my genes, encoded and evolved over thousands of generations of plant-loving ancestors. Maybe I am moved by happy memories of gardening from my childhood, when my favorite aunt invited me to help plant and harvest vegetables. Whatever the underlying cause (or causes), I've come to realize that I am far from alone in my positive emotional response to being in a garden. Feeling connected to plants in such a setting seems as natural to me as laughter, tears, and smiles. It's a powerful force that transcends the many differences among people on this planet. No matter where and how I've encountered this phenomenon, communion with nature always seems to deepen people's sense of spiritual well-being.

In order to better understand my fascination with the profound and soulful relationship between people and their gardens, it is helpful to know a little about me. I am a collector and a teller of stories. Since the 1970s, through two books and the medium of public radio, I've gathered and shared the true-life tales of hundreds of remarkable people. I've interviewed the rich and famous, the impoverished and unknown. I've taken my microphone and tape recorder to big cities, to small towns, and to farmhouses out in the country. It has even accompanied me into the coal mines of Colorado.

During my years as a radio journalist, I found myself most intrigued by folks who are not necessarily celebrities or high achievers, but who feed their souls through activities that hold deep meaning for them.

Some of these people are involved in creative pursuits that are commonly associated with muse and spirit—such as painting or poetry—while others derive special meaning from activities that may seem mundane. I have met quilters, for example, who appear to extract as much gratification from the making of a quilt as a Buddhist derives from Zen meditation. I'm not talking about exactly the same rewards, mind you, but a deeply spiritual connection nonetheless. These connections may be unconscious and even unsuspected, but they have the capacity to bring about great inner peace.

As I've grown older, gardens have attracted me more and more. If I'm dealing with loss or pain or am having an unusually challenging or stressful day, I find myself inexorably drawn to the quiet beauty of a garden.

Over the years, I've discovered that human inner growth is often stimulated or inspired by nature's outer growth. One spring day, back when I was living in the Upper Midwest, I was checking my flower garden in the backyard. It had been an unusually harsh winter—full of blizzards and below-zero temperatures—and the task at hand was depressing. I encountered one plant after another that had been completely devastated by the cold arctic winds. For most of these plants, I knew that there was no hope. They were dead and gone. After an hour, I was so bereft that tears were streaming down my cheeks. I felt that I had lost many of my oldest and dearest friends in this tragic natural disaster. Then, as I was about to give up all hope of finding a survivor, I stumbled upon the green shoot of a tiny red tulip pushing bravely through a hard crust of ice-heaved earth and waving its fat closed bud toward the sun like a triumphant victory flag. In an instant, my tears of sorrow became tears of joy. What a miracle to see this bright badge of color shining valiantly in a barren landscape of death and destruction. It was a transformative moment in which I fully understood the enormous power of healing and renewal that silently waits for me in my garden. The life force that fuels every plant and animal on our green planet was evident in that single audacious flower. My spirit soared and my view of the world shifted. I've never looked at a garden—or a tulip—in the same way since.

This change in perception and consciousness has frequently been expressed by the hundreds of gardeners I've interviewed. Whether they are summer vegetable growers or bonsai tree–shapers or balcony dabblers with petunias in clay pots, these folks see miracles unfolding every day. They talk about God's face shining in the unfurling of a flower, wildflowers unexpectedly appearing after a soaking thunderstorm, and the alchemy of kitchen scraps becoming fertile soil in the backyard compost pile. When I ask gardeners to reflect on these experiences, they're often disclosed through quiet musings and thoughtful reflections, revelations that might not be made until and unless I initiate a discussion of the metaphysics of gardening.

In the course of hundreds of interviews, I've never heard two gardeners express precisely the same sentiments. Everyone seems to have a different set of favorite associations with their plants. For example, writer Alfred Austin says that "being happy [in the garden] is getting dirt under your finger-nails, wearing old clothes, having a good idea get better the longer you work at it, starting a new flower bed, giving plants away, and listening to the rain."

I think most gardeners can relate to Austin's feelings, although their specific pleasures may vary. Even nongarden-ers have experienced the happy contentment he is describing: a sense of well-being associated with full absorption in a favorite pastime.

"I like sitting in a garden and smoking a good cigar," declared a sixty-three-year-old musician I met in one of New York City's pocket-size parks. "I am filled with a wonderful feeling of peace when I behold the unique beauty of each individual flower."

It is a special moment when backyard and park-bench con-versations move beyond the practical realm of trellises and seed catalogs to the transcendental rewards of tending the earth and admiring the flowers. When I listen carefully, I hear comments that are surprisingly heartfelt and deeply pro found. These observations have irrevocably changed the way I experience gardening, which is why I decided to share them with you in this book.

"You can learn a lot about yourself and your needs from your garden," my friend Bonnie assured me during a conver-sation we enjoyed in her leafy California yard. "That's why I wonder about someone who is seemingly unaware of his or her natural environment. Such people baffle me because I think something in us really needs to connect with nature. I worry that these folks don't nurture themselves. I believe that denying themselves connection with nature can cause a great deal of alienation on many levels. Myself, I feel very connected to plants and to the soil. I'm not a religious person at all, but there's something deeply spiritual to me about that link."

The connection Bonnie described is something I've always felt intuitively when I've been around flowers and plants, particularly those that I've grown myself. I also believe that not everyone is in touch with such feelings, perhaps because they've moved through human-shaped environments devoid of plants for much of their lives. They're not aware of what they're missing because they've never experienced nature directly. One of my goals in writing this book is to help you, as the reader, vicariously commune with the natural world through the experiences described by others. Whatever your background, I'm hopeful that their words will inspire you to make "the connection" on your own.

My backyard conversation with Bonnie about nature's transformative powers reminds me of an observation by the nineteenth-century American philosopher and essayist Ralph Waldo Emerson, who once described a walk in the "eternal calm" of sky and woods as "medicinal," restoring the tone of body and mind. Through such experiences, wrote Emerson, we find and renew ourselves again and again. More than a century later, studies by psychologists have confirmed that natural settings may be the most powerful antidote to mental fatigue yet found. Through my interviews with scores of serene gardeners, I'm more convinced than ever that this is true. What's more, gardening rests on a foundation of faith: a conviction that the miracles of nature will continue to unfold and abide in our universe before and after our mortal presence. "Even if I knew that tomorrow the world would go to pieces," theologian Martin Luther wrote, "I would still plant my apple tree." It is this faith in the mysteries of life that helps sustain us on our planet and makes us fully human.

"Our relationship with plants has the capacity to transform us," my neighbor Anna told me one sunny afternoon, as we strolled among her blooming snapdragons. "Plants help us become stronger and more self-aware. They also turn our world into a wonderful, magical, beautiful place, which is a very special thing."

Anna believes nature has the power to affect us in other important ways. "For example, the garden brings us the essence of peace. It teaches us some of the many rewards of being alone and of being quiet."

Surrounded by the exquisite splendor of Anna's healthy, well-tended garden, it was impossible to miss the almost palpable "soul energy" moving like an electric current between us and Anna's plants. I could not explain this tingling interaction scientifically; it seemed to be happening on a strictly intuitive and nonverbal level. Yet there it was, as real as the hummingbirds darting among the red-orange tubes of honeysuckle blossoms.

"We are living in a very sterile, artificial world, almost totally removed from nature," Anna observed. "As I drive through big cities, I see the concrete-and-steel environment that so many people are cooped up in all day long. We are so fortunate that plants have the capacity to put us right back in touch with the natural world, which we are always a fundamental part of as human beings. Even if it's unconscious, humans have a need for daily contact with something more substantial than the paper, computers, and TV screens that dominate our offices. Even something as simple as walking into a nursery or browsing through a garden center can help meet that need within us."

After my visit with Anna, I thought a lot about what she had told me. I knew that my friend had hit on a very important truth, one that is too rarely acknowledged publicly in our acquisitive, technology-driven culture. We need contact with nature in order to remain healthy, mentally as well as physically and spiritually.

A prolonged separation from nature may explain why I find myself looking out the window in the middle of a particularly frustrating day at the computer, feeling momentarily renewed by the gardens and landscaping I can see from my second-floor apartment. As I am writing this, I notice that the trees outside my apartment building have grown unusually lush from the record-breaking rains of winter. When I peer out the windows of my home office, I see only bright, fresh leaves dappled with filtered sunlight. I feel as though I'm in the middle of a cozy, green cocoon.

It strikes me as ironic—and a little tragic—that so many of us intentionally embrace a fast-paced, action-packed lifestyle that pulls us away from experiences that could feed our souls simply and directly. We spend many hours each week trying—often unsuccessfully—to make our lives full and happy, when a sense of well-being and contentment may be as near as our backyard, the public garden down the street, or among the leaves aflutter just beyond our windowsill.

Not all people choose to live this way. In Houston, I met Judy, a plant-lover who had grown up in a tiny Texas town that was much too small to have a municipal park. Judy's great-grandfather, a German immigrant, spoke almost no English when he moved to the town.

"Great-Grandpa was a truck farmer and gardener who sold produce door-to-door from the back of his mule-drawn wagon," said Judy, smiling at the distant but vivid memory of this humble man. "He provided many of the fresh fruits and vegetables for town residents, but what they appreciated most was his skill in pruning topiary shapes out of hedges and shrubs. After a few years, Great-Grandpa had carved the images of dozens of animals in the yards of his neighbors, which made the whole town look like a park. Everyone appreciated the way he turned their gardens into something special."

The folksy friendliness and slow pace that allowed the work of such gardeners to flourish are hard to find now; yet even the busiest among us are able to find a time and place to connect with nature if we so desire.

Peter, an aggressive, thirty-something, Chicago business executive, told me that gardening is his favorite way to relax after a hard day at the office. "When I'm puttering around in my garden, I experience a marvelous sort of 'conscious unconsciousness.' It's a feeling of being tremendously engaged in what I'm doing while also remaining detached. I get a similar feeling when I'm playing the piano—as if I'm a part of what's going on but also not a part. My usual worries and cares evaporate when I garden and I feel in tune with the natural order of things, which is very comforting."

Peter also confessed that gardening brings out his gentle and nurturing side, traits that don't get much support in the competitive world of work. Others have told me similar stories of how their gardens provide them with a chance to be generous.

"I give away most of the things that I grow," conceded my friend Audrey, who touches the lives of nearly everyone in her neighborhood with her bounty. "People come by and they ask me, 'Do you have any mint? Do you have some basil? Do you have this, do you have that?' There is such a pleasure in being able to give, and there is something about growing a plant all by myself that refreshes the soul. Growing something means seeing the miracle of life unfold before my eyes, and I love to share that with people."

A garden can be a place of solace, a soothing oasis away from humanity and a refuge from the demands of the world. In Nashville, I interviewed Evelyn, a lifelong gardener in her sixties who had recently lost her husband to cancer.

"A garden can heal the spirit," said Evelyn, in a gentle but resolute voice. "My plants got me through my sadness after my husband died—I couldn't have made it without them. I consider my garden to be a private place, a place of great tranquillity. When I want to be alone or with one of my special friends, the garden is the place I go. It's my escape from the world.

"The garden teaches us that everything has a season and that there is a time to linger as well as a time to move on. You also learn that when spring comes, flowers will soon bloom again. We can depend on that—and I feel that we need to depend on it."

Evelyn is a strong believer in the old adage that one is closer to God in a garden than anywhere else on Earth. The deep spiritual connection she feels with her plants is a great source of comfort and invariably brings Evelyn a feeling of inner peace.

"I love having flowers in the house," she told me, nodding in the direction of a vase filled with calla lilies. "Flowers change the way a house feels. They are truly food for the soul. I also learn patience from my garden. I learn to adjust to its pace. Once I sat completely still and watched a flower open. It was quite magical."

Sometimes the magic of her garden inspires Evelyn to write poetry. Her primary desire is not to have these personal poems published or widely read but rather to capture in verse the unique feelings the garden evokes within her heart. She conceded that while hers may not be great poetry, such musings allow her to express more fully the joys and insights of gardening. I've included a sample from Evelyn—and, later on, some lines from other amateur poets—because I agree that some emotions are better expressed in verse than prose:

SPRING SONG

Warmed by midday sun,
The brown earth crumbles through my fingers,
Embracing seed with promises of all that the
    harvest brings.
Soft winds caress,
The sound of muffled drums,
And high above my head a mockingbird sings.

Although I am not a poet, I admire those who can string together lines that capture experience and feeling with such economy and beauty. Words like these have the power to unlock emotions and the storehouse of our most treasured memories. I relate completely to what Evelyn expressed in this poem. When she first recited "Spring Song" to me, I was reminded of a garden that I grew and tended shortly after my first son was born, half a lifetime ago. My husband and I were sharing our first house together and we were thrilled with the prospect of making it a comfortable home of our own. And for me, no house was truly a home without a green lawn in front and flowerbeds overflowing with the familiar petunias, hostas, pansies, hollyhocks, and zinnias of my childhood.

The sight of these welcoming summertime flowers cheered me whenever my husband and I pulled into the driveway or I looked out the kitchen window while washing dishes. But what surprised and delighted me most was the way I felt when I actually worked in this garden, on my knees with fingers plunged into the rich, loamy soil. In those moments, I sensed an abiding calm and an appreciation for the way in which my life was in tune with the cycles of the earth. I saw the whole universe in a microcosm: plants being born, maturing, reproducing, dying, and decaying into the components of soil. I knew that I was as much as part of these cycles as they were, and I felt a contentment in that knowledge.

"The garden gives me an inner peace," a Los Angeles gardener named Iris confided to me many years later, and I knew exactly what she meant.

"I always found when I was ill," Iris continued, "that when I was able to get out in the garden and put my hands into the soil, I was rejuvenated. Think about it. What is there in the stuff we call 'earth' that helps a plant grow? It must be alive with all kinds of things or how else could a seed ever germinate? When I garden, that very aliveness comes into my spirit and gives me something back."

The nurturing of the spirit that Iris experienced—and that I certainly felt in the garden of my first home—can really feed our souls. I'm convinced that it's one of the main reasons people are attracted to gardening, although this awareness may never reach a conscious level. I also believe this is why many city dwellers, who may not tend any plants of their own, are drawn so powerfully to urban parks and public gardens.

"You can feel the energy of gardens," a busy New Yorker named Sonja told me during our brief encounter in one of Manhattan's many public gardens. "They have a magical, mystical feeling."

Sonja likes to sit among the flowers during breaks in her work or as a respite from weekend errand running around the city.

"Flowers are beautiful," she told me, "and you can't duplicate their colors in anything man-made. Maybe the difference is the light. I'm sure that the light shining on a flower does something to the energy of the plants."

Sonja said she gets "dreamy" on May afternoons when many of New York City's parks are overflowing with bright blossoms: "I love to see pinks and lavenders and magentas together. Pinks and purples are an especially wonderful combination. I think the colors make me happy and that certainly makes my day at work a lot easier."

Another garden visitor, who introduced herself as Elizabeth, eavesdropped on our conversation and volunteered an opinion of her own. "People are trying to find a balance in their lives," she speculated, "and gardening helps them feel centered. You don't have to think about anything when you're out admiring a garden; you can enter a state of absolute bliss. This is one of the only activities in our busy modern society where it's acceptable to do that."

According to Sonja, gardeners are the planet's oldest souls, the ones who are the most in touch with the mysteries of the earth. I found myself seconding her opinion that gardening is a sacred act, a mutual nurturing of human and earth that dates back to prehistoric times. Elizabeth chimed in once more, wondering aloud whether schools should be required to teach children how to grow plants, along with reading, writing, and arithmetic. "Maybe the crime rate would go down," she ventured, "if we all grew up nurturing tiny seeds and flowers."

It may seem odd to talk about gardens while one is surrounded by the unholy din of midday Manhattan traffic. Odd, I agree, yet entirely appropriate. What could be more normal—and necessary—than celebrating the simple miracles of life in an environment where nature has been almost entirely replaced by concrete, steel, and asphalt? The rarer gardens become, I mused, the more we need them. This is why I am always encouraging people to cultivate plants, even if they are hemmed in by loud streets and tall skyscrapers. You can always find room to grow something on a windowsill, in a

flowerpot, or beneath a skylight. Wherever you find the nourishing glow of sunshine, you can cultivate a plant.

Marcia, a self-described "fire-escape gardener" in a big East
Coast city, told me that time spent among the potted plants
in her miniature garden is "wonderfully soul-satisfying."

"There is something so marvelous about working in a place
that is so beautiful," she stressed. "In the middle of a bad day,
even looking at pictures in a seed catalog feels terrific." When
she peers out the window at her chrysanthemums, Marcia
tunes out the honking horns and wailing sirens that drift up
from seven stories below.

Suburbanites, too, derive these kinds of satisfactions from
their gardens. My friend Jonathon is an ambitious baby
boomer who downshifted from the fast-lane lifestyle of his
high-stress jobs in New York and Los Angeles into the com-
parative calm of a spacious office in downtown Minneapolis.
He commutes four days a week from a comfortable home on
a nearby lake and spends many hours with his wife puttering
around their large garden.

"I'm convinced that the forces bringing overloaded, hard-
working people like me to gardening in midlife are the same
things that are bringing them to spiritualism," Jonathon
declared as we relaxed in the shadow of tall trees that form a
semicircle in his backyard. "Gardening is part of my search for
inner peace, because I really do feel at one with the plants that
I'm tending. It's such a peaceful, beautiful, and natural thing
to do.

"Another great satisfaction of gardening is that one can see
progress, and in most of the things we do in our lives—

including the work at our jobs—we see little or no progress of any kind. Expectations can be met by a garden, and that's a very healthy, rewarding thing for any of us to experience."

I asked Jonathon to speculate on why an increasing number of his peers—members of the generation born during the two decades following World War II—have embraced gardening with such passion. His thoughtful reply resonated with comments I've heard from gardeners of all ages.

"Baby boomers are searching for some kind of deep spiritual meaning," said Jonathon. "We want some kind of anchor in our lives. In a small way, a garden provides this. There is a genuine inner peace that can be found and enjoyed by virtue of tending one's plants. You can see real growth and exquisite beauty that you create with your own hands and head and heart. We're living in a time of terrible inner turmoil, and many of us feel that our society is a spiritual desert that has become pretty barren of meaning. Gardening is enormously satisfying when so many domains of our lives offer nothing that feels stationary or solid.

"The garden has taught me a patience about change and a reverence for Earth that I was too busy to notice before, scurrying from one airplane and one phone call to the next. I never really noticed the true beauty of nature before I started gardening. For many, many reasons, I think gardening is one of the most kind and useful things that people can do for themselves as well as for our Earth."

For Jonathon, the garden is a teacher of simple yet important truths. As we grow older and change, these teachings and truths shift to meet different needs. Through all the phases and dimensions of our lives, a garden is there to nurture us whenever we are ready.

"My garden and my feelings about gardening evolve over time," explained Daniel, a baby boomer who tends a half-acre yard in Wisconsin. "Sometimes this means learning to love and appreciate a plant I thought that I hated."

When I asked him to clarify this statement, Daniel told me about a strongly opinionated friend who flatly announced one day, "I simply can't stand petunias!" This straight-laced fellow didn't like to take chances with unruly flowers that might easily get out of control or that are too boisterous and showy in their beauty.

"But not long afterward, this same friend saw a petunia used as part of a very creative design in someone else's garden, and he began to look at that sort of simple, carefree plant in an entirely new way. The next thing you know, this guy tells me that he actually *likes* petunias."

Daniel described another outspoken and control-oriented friend who toured Daniel's garden one day and asked, in a very emphatic and negative tone of voice, "What is *that* flower?" The man was pointing at an old-fashioned hollyhock, which was blooming with undisciplined and unabashed extravagance. The visitor softened after Daniel named the plant and then murmured, "You know, my grandfather grew those in his garden out behind the barn." A few weeks later, Daniel's uptight pal had half a dozen hollyhocks outside his own home. Before that, an exuberant hollyhock would have had no business in the formality and stateliness of the man's garden. "These two experiences," Daniel concluded, "remind me that things are awakened in us as new perspectives come into view, as the garden awakens and stimulates our senses afresh."

Daniel and Jonathon spoke of feeling spiritually enriched and enlivened through their connections with the earth. Both men found it easier to see "the big picture" of life when they focused on the small-scale world of their gardens. They are among a growing number of individuals for whom gardening provides an opportunity for contemplation and prayer. It isn't only baby boomers and younger folks who feel this way. Older gardeners, in particular, have told me that they use their gardens as a refuge for quiet reflection, for solitude, and for opening their hearts.

"I approach gardening as a time for meditation, as a time to be by myself, and as a time to share emotions," said Gil, a soft-spoken retired businessman who was in his sixties at the time of our interview. "I love to experience the exuberance of fresh, colorful flowers, the newness that I encounter at every turn in my garden."

For Gil, much of the passion for gardening comes from learning to be flexible with nature and to live with compromise. "I know that I must have patience with my plants and that I must accept failure among them as well as successes. The garden never lets me become arrogant of triumphs—at least not for long. I have learned to appreciate the wonderful balance that exists throughout nature and the crucial fact that there is a balance. My garden teaches me this again and again."

For those who are religious in a more traditional sense of the word, gardening may be a kind of showcase for God's miracles and mercy. It can be a place where communication with the

Creator is both personal and direct. In Nashville, for example, I spent a delightful afternoon in the company of a devout Christian woman who tended one of the loveliest gardens I'd ever seen.

"My garden is really the place to be if you want to get in touch with God," Geneva told me, as we sipped fresh lemonade in the modest bungalow she occupies in an old, tree-shaded neighborhood. "You're away from distractions, your thoughts are clear, and you can talk to the Lord exactly the way you want to talk to him. You can sit quietly and meditate. You can make your plans and ask him to help you succeed in carrying out those plans. This is where it all happens for me: in the garden."

I asked Geneva to give me a specific example of how spending time in her garden influences her daily life. She stared into the distance for a moment, then turned toward me and spoke in a soft voice thick with emotion. I knew from an earlier conversation that she had been distraught over the recent death of a close friend whom she'd known for many years.

"I noticed yesterday that I didn't have a chance to go out in the garden before I left the house. And, you know, I felt so sad. I had some business with my banker, and at the end of our meeting, I finally told him, 'I've been crying a lot today. Don't worry, George, I'm okay. But I really have to get this meeting out of the way so that I can get back into my garden.' This morning I went outside, bright and early. That's why I'm smiling now: because I feel so much better.

"There really is a sense of healing when you go into a garden. Sometimes you don't have to think about anything at all;

simply being out there helps you. That's why sometimes I choose to sit in the garden, close my eyes, and meditate. On these occasions I don't want to go anywhere else, I don't want to do anything else, I just want to be in my garden. Sometimes it's important to relax both the mind and the body, and my garden is a place where I can always do that."

Geneva and I agreed that a garden is not only a serene and restful place but also a wise and eye-opening teacher. A garden's plants show us the unfolding of every stage of life: the beginning, middle, and end.

"You can see parallels in your own existence," said Geneva. "We all grow from tiny seeds, just as plants do. We have the capacity to flourish and to spread joy through our presence, like our gardens."

Geneva feels sorry for some of her older neighbors who have lost interest in their gardens or never had it to begin with. "Gardening is so much more satisfying than sitting at home doing nothing. As we tend our gardens we are full of life and can really enjoy our maturity and richness, just as plants do. We learn how humans need the same kind of nourishment that all other living things need. Plants give and receive tender loving care, exactly like a person does, and both flourish when they get the right kind of attention."

When Geneva said this, I thought about times in my life when I've felt unloved or neglected and how the tending of plants helped fill the hole in my heart. I remembered how satisfying it was to coax a bud to open on a plant that I'd rescued from certain death with fertilizer, water, sunlight, and words of encouragement. Flowers and plants have always been a soothing balm for my soul during turmoil and trouble. I instinctively turn to them for reassurance in times of stress or crisis.

"Explain to me," I asked Geneva, "how gardening nourishes you." She examined her fingers for a moment, then spread her palms toward me, as if offering me a gift.

"When my hands are in the dirt and I'm growing something on the outside," said Geneva, "I'm growing on the inside too. There's such a deep, relaxed feeling within me when I'm working with plants. I know that I'm being nurtured when I'm interacting with the earth. In my own garden, I believe that I'm expanding and flourishing in many of the same ways that my plants are."

On the flight back to Los Angeles from Nashville, I thought about my conversation with Geneva. Her enthusiastic and intimate relationship with her plants brought to mind an interview I had conducted with an entirely different sort of gardener, one who views gardening as a creative act and a garden as a work of art. Melva is a middle-aged painter who tends a half-acre garden at her home near Saint Paul, Minnesota. A bundle of energy who greets her visitors with a warm hug, Melva immediately gave me an in-depth tour of her yard and talked about the many ways her garden inspires her.

"I'm out as early as I can be," she confided. "My husband, Bill, says he calls me in for lunch, and then he calls me in for dinner, and then he says, 'Honey, aren't you gonna come in tonight?' And when I finally do come in, he says, 'You just stand at the door and look out.'"

Melva is lucky to have a partner as good natured and as

indulgent as Bill. Yet he admits to benefiting from his wife's obsession in a number of unexpected ways.

"One night recently I had to call Bill out of the house to watch a particularly gorgeous sunset with me," said Melva. "If I hadn't been in the garden, I'd never have noticed it, and yet that sunset had qualities that could never be described in words or captured in a photograph. It was like the most spectacular work of art, very feathered-over and abstract looking.

"I definitely view my garden as a form of artistic expression. It's almost like a living, ongoing sculpture. It never looks the same two days in a row. For example, it can seem unsightly, and all of a sudden, there's this beautiful little iris blooming in a corner that I never noticed before. Things like that are just so amazing—they make all the work worthwhile, and they make my garden feel very sacred."

It was obvious that her garden is a tremendous source of joy and renewal for Melva. She makes time each day to linger among her flowers and to witness the changes unfolding in the natural environment she so lovingly maintains. Like me, Melva relies on her garden for a daily dose of optimism and delight. I was happy to learn that she's passing her upbeat outlook on to the younger generation.

"I even take my eighteen-month-old grandson, Eric, out in the garden when he comes over to visit me and my husband," laughed Melva. "This little boy and I say 'hello' to iris and 'hello' to poppy, and I pull the plants over to Eric so he can bury his face in them. I can't imagine not having a garden, and I'm determined to let all of my grandchildren know how much gardening can mean to them."

When we were finished with the grand tour, Melva and I sat silently for a few minutes and absorbed the summertime sounds of her garden. Crickets chirped merrily, a mockingbird trilled, and honeybees buzzed from one nectar-filled blossom to another. Melva gave me a knowing smile. Then I asked her what lessons she thinks that tending this special piece of earth teaches her.

"Gardening teaches me to listen," Melva replied, touching an index finger to the middle of her chin. "It teaches me to hear the birds and the crickets and the rustle of the leaves. It teaches me to see—to watch the sky and to notice how the shadows change during the course of the day. My very awareness of everything around me is heightened when I spend time outdoors.

"I also feel melancholy in the garden sometimes. After a while, you just know when the flowers are about to shrivel and fade away. It's hard for me, in the early spring, to know that it will be a year before I enjoy the jonquils again. I look at them and think, *Golly, I won't see you for such a long while.* It's as if part of my life is going with them. I equate that with the process of letting go of those we love most, which is something we are always faced with, aren't we?"

Melva's final comment was particularly significant to me. As I've grown older, I've learned how important it is to accept the inevitable losses that all of us encounter in the course of our lives. This includes the harsh but inevitable reality of the death of loved ones.

Each of the world's major religions makes a special effort to help us learn to let go of that which is dearest to us, and each refers to the garden as a place of refuge and renewal. Such sacred scriptures as the Bible and the Koran are sprinkled with references to nature as a teacher of fundamental human truths.

The biblical book Ecclesiastes, for example, declares that "to everything, there is a season," while Revelation advises: "Hurt not the earth, neither the sea nor the trees." One of the most well-known New Testament passages praises the simple miracles of nature: "Consider the lilies of the field, how they grow; they toil not, neither do they spin: And yet I say unto you, that even Solomon in all his glory was not arrayed like one of these."

In the Jewish tradition, the Chassidic mystic Rabbi Nachman of Breslov reflected on nature in his *Outpouring of the Soul:*

> How wonderful it would be if one could only be worthy of hearing the song of the grass. Each blade of grass sings out to God without any ulterior motive and without expecting any reward. It is most wonderful to hear its song and worship God in its midst. The best place to meditate is in a field where things grow. There one can truly express his thoughts before God.

As part of the religion of Islam, the holy teachings of the Koran define *paradise* as a garden flowing with milk, honey, wine, and water. The word itself derives from the Persian term for "walled garden," which in the Middle East is often planted with fruit or nut trees, palms, pines, and cypresses that symbolize both death and eternal life.

"Every religion has its gardens," Harry (Rick) Moody, philosopher and coauthor of *The Five Stages of the Soul,* noted in an interview. "They point back to something primordial, making a two-way connection to beauty, mercy, and grace. We need gardens and they need us; it's a gift in both directions."

Through my conversations with gardeners, I've discovered that tending plants is definitely an interactive process. For example, a garden can help ease the sorrow of loss by providing personal associations that nurture our memories of the deceased. While I was visiting friends and family in Minnesota, I spent part of an afternoon with John, a fortyish newspaper reporter who had lost both parents the previous year.

"I bring geraniums into my formal living room for the winter," John told me, making a sweeping gesture with his right arm in the direction of the red and pink blossoms bathed in the sunlight of a picture window. "I think it's because my father always over-wintered his geraniums in his house. They don't really go with any of my decor, but somehow I have a compulsion to go through this ritual. Because I inherited some cuttings from my dad, I now have some lovely descendants of geraniums that, for all I know, could be twenty or thirty years old."

John said that one of the most important lessons he learned from his mother and father is to always focus on the "journey" that underlies life's activities, not simply on the "arrival."

"My parents' lives were very small in terms of geography," he continued, "yet Mom and Dad had a very big impact on their community. It wasn't a matter of having accomplished any grand deeds during their lives, but of always having had the time—and the fresh vegetables or cuttings from ornamental plants—to share with their neighbors."

After his mother and father died, John sorted through his parents' belongings and eventually sold the family home, but not before he unburied a few living treasures from the soil.

"The last thing I did before the new owners arrived was dig a few special plants out of the ground: Mom's favorite lemon lily and a trillium, along with one of Dad's favorite purple lilacs. They are now here in full evidence, in my garden, where they are deeply appreciated. So for the past few years I've enjoyed the physical evidence of the wonderful heritage that was my parents' garden."

Virtually every one of us can make similar associations between certain loved ones and their favorite plants. I can't look at pansies, for example, without thinking of a close friend who is filled with delight whenever she sees a bed filled with their happy, colorful faces in the otherwise drab months of late winter. Another friend has had a lifelong love affair with the purple blossoms of wisteria vines, and I can't encounter these extravagant and heavily scented flowers without remembering the way my pal Debora shouts with joy every time she sees them.

One of the wonderful things about plants, as my neighbor Barbara has pointed out, is that they are so simple and unpretentious. They are 100 percent what they are, no more and no less.

"Simply being is the only thing that they do," Barbara

pointed out one day, after I'd taken a walk and stopped to admire her rosebushes. "They remind me that there is a particular kind of tending and nurturing that they need just as my heart and my relationships need tending and nurturing in order for me to feel at ease, to feel safe, and to feel fully loved."

With the passage of time, I have a better sense of what my neighbor was talking about. If you're like me, it's always the little things in a relationship with a spouse, child, or friend that help me feel loved and appreciated on a daily basis. This nurturing may come through an unexpected compliment or a kind word, a spontaneous hug or a thoughtful gift, an intimate conversation or a funny story. I'm sure plants feel the same sort of uplift when we feed them, give them a drink, remove dead leaves, and protect them from their enemies. When we do this, it gives our plants a chance to fully celebrate their true essence.

Barbara feels that "all plants have a very clear sense of who and what they are. I believe their purpose is simply to be beautiful and to manifest themselves in the world as the plants they are meant to be. Roses love to be roses. You can count on them to always bloom into the most radiant flowers. A rose has no interest in being a chrysanthemum, which is why it does 'rose-ing' so very well and doesn't do 'chrysanthemuming' at all."

For Barbara, gardening is simply part of the normal, everyday rhythm of life. It includes moments of drudgery and disappointment as well as of joy and laughter. She feels frustrated with her garden at times, but this is balanced by its enormous capacity to create satisfaction and pleasure.

Barbara's garden has taught her to pay attention in the face of distraction and to keep her own life in balance.

"If I get too busy," she conceded, "one of my little green friends withers away and drops out. I've learned to accept that, just as I've learned to bring my changing moods to the garden. Sometimes I turn music on, and I dance and sing while I'm doing my gardening. Other times I am quiet, and gardening becomes like meditation for me, a way to express the sense of honor that I have for the earth and the way it tends and nurtures me in return."

My neighbor is like me in that every home she has ever lived in has been shared with plants. The size, number, and type of plants change depending on circumstance, but their presence is a constant. I've had carefully manicured flower beds when I was first married, for example, followed by backyards that were sacrificed to play areas when I had three kids under the age of five. As I've grown older, my garden has shrunk to a few houseplants and a balcony filled with pots, yet my emotional bond with gardening is as strong as ever. My fellow gardeners express this connection better than I can.

"I really want something that is living, breathing, authentic, and growing in my immediate vicinity," Barbara told me while she tenderly stroked the feathery needles of a Norfolk Island pine. "I'm sure that I need them as much as they need me. They feed my soul.

"You must learn to trust in the awesome power of nature if you're going to succeed with plants," she continued. "This process is very exhilarating, and one is always rewarded by the plants' exquisite beauty."

When we nurture and pay attention to plants—or, for that matter, anything in nature—we allow ourselves to become partners in the complex web of ongoing processes that sustain our very lives. This is both exciting and empowering. Through such interactions we learn to respect not only the awesome power and beauty of nature, but also our own human abilities. The result is a kind of anxiety-free concentration that can liberate us from our daily litany of cares and woes.

My friend Ketzel Levine, a devoted horticulturist and gardening writer, likes to equate the garden with serenity. "Gardeners give up all their preoccupations and focus solely on their actions, their labor," she points out. "It's very freeing in that respect because you're concentrating entirely on tending, nurturing, growing, and caring for your plants.

"My head empties out when I garden. When that happens I am nothing except another force of nature. Gardening eliminates a great deal of the trouble and turmoil in my mind because it focuses my energy on doing one simple activity. The pleasures of the garden become so simple and so focused that aesthetics take on new meaning. A flowering del phinium, for example, can become an absolutely perfect vision of loveliness."

Ketzel dispenses plant-care advice on public radio and operates her own landscaping business in Portland, Oregon. She's answered thousands of questions about gardening over the years, often explaining to exasperated novice gardeners that there's a limit to how far nature can be bent to follow their wills.

"With plants, there are so many things that are simply out of your control. You can do some things to tend and nurture your plants, but you have no control over what happens to them. You can't stop the wind, the rain, the nematodes, the voles, or any other scourge. Nature is ultimately in control, a truth that applies to our own lives as well."

Ketzel's practical, no-nonsense approach to gardening is based on years of daily experience with every kind of plant grown in all kinds of conditions. Her conclusions reflect the pragmatism learned by any close observer of nature.

"The dynamics of the garden are basic," she said. "Plants die on you and they thrive on you. They may never talk back, but they inevitably let you know how they feel. There are no politics in a garden, no controversy. Your interaction with a plant is a very singular relationship that's completely of your own making. In the garden, you explore yourself and your creativity, your tolerance, your madness, your obsessiveness, your level of concentration, your level of caring. There is no competition in gardening, except with yourself."

I asked Ketzel's opinion on why gardening is so popular in a modern and affluent society where we can buy fresh produce at a market, order flowers over the telephone, and have someone come in once a week to tend our yard. It would appear that anyone can enjoy all the tangible rewards of a garden without ever having to lift a watering can.

"The tangible rewards are not at issue," Ketzel replied, leaning forward to drive home her point. "In some sense, gardening deals with mortality. It's our attempt to leave our mark, to make a difference on our planet Earth, to say, 'I was here, and I created this!' Although they may start gardening for very practical reasons, what motivates most people to stick with it has little to do with practicality."

For example, Ketzel uses gardening as a stepping-stone into silent absorption, away from the noises of the world as well as the inner distractions of her busy life. "For the most part, gardening is about solitude," she reminded me. "And gardening can make solitude feel like solace instead of the prison it is for some people.

"Finally, there is a constant process of renewal that is always visible among plants, which means that when you're a gardener there is always hope. The magnificent thing about a garden is that it is never, ever the same from one hour to the next. The light, the wind, the angle of the plants' leaves, the energy levels—they're always changing."

By coincidence, Ketzel's comments echoed those of another gardener I had interviewed the previous day in Seattle.

"Everything grows and changes in a garden," Daphne had told me. "Try to hold on to a beautiful blossom and it changes, almost as you're watching it. Create the perfect design and it achieves its own perfection that wasn't what you had in mind, or the seeds you planted never come up, or they come up in different places than where you sowed them."

I don't think it was simple coincidence that brought such similar points of view into my life within the space of twenty-four hours. The life lessons that Ketzel and Daphne described are similar to those that many gardeners have talked about during subsequent interviews with me. What each of these gardeners has in common is an abiding acceptance of the fact that although every living organism is in a constant state of change, the natural cycle of that change has a predictability that includes birth, growth, maturity, decline, and death. And, after death, the mortal remains of that organism become energy to sustain the next sequence of life-forms. When humans accept this universal cycle, they are in greater harmony with Earth.

An activity that supports a harmonious relationship with our planet is something that therapist and writer Ruth Baetz calls "communing with nature." In her book *Wild Communion,* Baetz offers suggestions on how a person may deepen his or her awareness of the natural world in order to feel a sense of fundamental connectedness—a primal "oneness"—with the universe. My experience has shown me that the same kinds of feelings of serenity, peacefulness, and bliss that Baetz experiences in national parks and wilderness areas can also be evoked by gardens large and small.

There is no right or wrong way to make the soul connection in a garden. The best approach for you may involve digging your fingers into the soil and working with plants directly. Or, you might feel just as connected when you admire the trees and flowers cultivated by a friend or neighbor. If you live in an urban setting, the connection could be made in a city park or a community garden. The choices are virtually endless, and you're sure to find one that feels appropriate to your needs, capabilities, and interests. In upcoming chapters, I'll discuss a variety of approaches that have been successful for the hundreds of garden-lovers I've interviewed.

No matter what our circumstances, I'm convinced that the human soul harbors a deep yearning for harmony with nature. Over the last few generations, as we have become more urban and technological, our species has begun to slip away from its strong bond with the earth. Yet I believe that a "heart connection" to plants (and other living things) is essential if our society is to remain in a healthy relationship with its natural environment. This is true whether we are nurturing plants in a tiny clay pot or on an acre of land, whether we are tending this greenery ourselves or admiring the gardens cared for by others. I am also convinced that our human family is being challenged to stop abusing the natural systems that keep our planet whole and healthy. We must end these abuses and begin healing the wounds humanity has inflicted on our fragile biosphere. Lovingly tending a garden may seem like a pitifully small step toward making a shift in global behavior, but I believe that the spiritual connection we make through such conscious action can put our hearts directly in touch with the very soul of Earth. It is through these soulful connections that our planet—and our lives— will change for the better. Indeed, philosophers, spiritual leaders, and social scientists argue that changes in the heart and in human consciousness yield the only meaningful shifts in behavior. It is through the actual experience of gardens and gardening, I believe, that a profound change occurs in our fundamental relationship with Earth and our active role in its future.

CHAPTER TWO

# The Wisdom of the Urban Gardener

Renewing our age-old bond with nature while surrounded by steel-and-glass skyscrapers and crowded
thoroughfares demands ingenuity, creativity, and per-
sistence. One must be armed with optimism and imagi-
nation to make a safe haven for thriving plants and
blooming flowers in a place where every square inch of
ground appears to be already spoken for.

—Mark, a gardener in New Mexico

I live in a city that has hundreds of tall buildings, thousands
of miles of paved roads, and an overabundance of concrete.
Millions of us call places like this our home, places in which
cement and asphalt have replaced the comforting and useful vegetation that nature once provided. Despite our artificial, human-made environment, many city dwellers—
including me—feel a strong impulse to find a compatible

35

balance between the stimulating urban atmosphere and the serene beauty of the natural world. Even in a high-rise apartment or crowded condo, there is always a way to dig your fingers into the soil and to nurture delicate growing things, even if it means sharing a plot in a community garden or perching your plants on a windowsill.

I have rented houses and apartments, for example, where the only "garden" I had was the collection of plants suspended from ceiling hooks. At other times in my life, I've cultivated big plots blessed with abundant sunshine and rich, loamy soil. As gardeners, we learn to make the best of what we're given. And, as this chapter illustrates, even modest resources can yield a great deal. Someone wise (and here anonymous) summed it up this way: "Our gardens are pockets where our creator keeps our dreams."

I was listening to my local public-radio station one Thanksgiving Day when I heard a story that was so arresting I had to stop preparing my pumpkin pie and pay complete attention to what was being said. A woman I'd never heard of was giving thanks for her experience as a "balcony gardener" in a multilevel apartment building. I was particularly moved by Hillary Nelson's description of how her tiny garden had changed the lives of her neighbors, who saw the flowery fire escape as a beacon of hope that brightened their difficult lives. When folks looked up from the grimy streets of Manhattan's Lower East Side, they glimpsed this woman's cheerful red roses on the wrought-iron balcony. For those few seconds, the world was a beautiful place.

I was so impressed with her remarkable experience that I

contacted Hillary Nelson and asked for her permission to publish "An Essay of Thanksgiving" in this book. I am very thankful that she has allowed me to share her heartwarming story with you:

I used to live in Hell's Kitchen in New York City, and that's where I learned how to garden. We lived on the third floor of a crumbling brownstone—the kind of place where the landlord has no phone number, just a post office box for the rent.

One day, some inept direct marketer sent me a flyer for mail-order roses. I looked out my window at the empty, forlorn lot below me and then sat down and ordered three rose bushes. They came about a week later, eighteen-inch thorny sticks in a plastic bag filled with soggy newspaper.

"What are you going to do with them?" my husband wanted to know. "Well," I answered, "we need to build a box about a foot and one-half deep and a foot wide, and then we'll hang it up outside the window and plant them."

"What we?" he asked, and started off for the lumberyard over on Tenth Avenue.

Filled with potting soil and roses, the window box weighed about three hundred pounds, and I was terrified that the people who lived downstairs might come out into their yard just in time to get flattened as the box pulled free of the deteriorating brick wall. But it hung in there, and in June, pink buds began to swell.

One Sunday, as we sat reading the *Times*, I suddenly smelled them—at least ten blossoms had burst open in the hot morning sun and sat blushing and nodding as a city breeze wafted their perfume, along with the sound of the M-11 bus, into our apartment.

Soon, wonderful things started happening to us. People would stop me on the street.

"I know you!" they'd exclaim. "You're the one with the flowers. Ooh, they are so very nice!"

The people would call up from Forty-eighth Street, "What are they?" "Roses!" we'd shout back. "Que bonita!" they'd yell. "Gracias!" we'd yell back.

Eventually, my first-floor neighbors moved out, and we grabbed their apartment sight unseen because those roses had made us so land hungry. I planted nicotiana and foxgloves, columbine and ferns, hellebores and viburnum, all of which could thrive in the dim light at the foot of the tenement. Woodpeckers visited, and hummingbirds the size of bumblebees; at night, bats swooped by, devouring mosquitoes and moths.

One morning, I found a local hooker-junkie asleep under the gardenia on a sheet she had swiped from my clothesline. She was very thin and her pale face was covered with welts, which meant she had AIDS. "You got a very nice yard," she remarked. "It don't smell like the city." As I led her out through the dingy hallway, she turned and said, "From here, you'd never know somethin' so nice was back there." She walked away swinging her skinny arms and singing cheerily.

About a year ago, we moved to New Hampshire, to a house built by the Shakers. From my kitchen, I can see a lilac bush planted 150 years ago. With all the windows shut against a cold spring night, its scent still fills the house.

I designed an elaborate garden made of boxed beds in geometric shapes, divided by gravel paths and with a tree at its center—a *potager* it's called, and it's based on the medieval gardens grown behind monastery walls.

Now, strangers often stop to admire my garden; they sometimes ask why I put a crab apple in the center, and I simply shrug my shoulders. But I will tell you why. I don't know if I believe in God, but I do believe in the Garden of Eden and every person's right to live there. And so I did not plant an apple tree—the symbol of man's fall—at the heart of my garden, as the monks would have done. Instead, I planted a crab apple, a smaller tree, one whose fruit is not big or sweet, but little and tart, and whose leaves shine such a clear and brilliant red in the autumn sun that they could stop your heart with their small, imperfect beauty.

It is our nature to find joy in unexpected places. Without this capacity, humankind would long ago have died out from sheer misery. I don't ever forget that there are hummingbirds in Hell's Kitchen, that roses grow on tenement balconies, and that a garden prompted a prostitute to sing. That is why I plant a garden. And that is why, today, I give thanks.

Hillary Nelson's essay is a wonderful reminder of the many ways in which gardening often touches the life not only of the gardener but also of many of his or her neighbors. This can—and does—happen in cities throughout the world.

"Do you see that big plant over there?" The little old man was pointing to a plot he was cultivating in one of the community gardens that now dot the boulevards of Brooklyn. "Can you believe that I grew that from a single seed! Now, when I walk along the sidewalks and look up at the windows, I see many flowers that bloom on cuttings taken from that same plant. It makes me feel proud to know that people are getting so much pleasure from something that I grew from a tiny seed."

Later that afternoon a woman I interviewed at a community garden on West Eighty-ninth Street in Manhattan told me that she has been stopping there nearly every day after work for seventeen years. "Walking through here is like therapy for me," she said. "This garden makes me and countless other people happy. It's a wonderful place for the whole community."

The next day, at a small, well-kept public garden not far from Central Park, I met Alice. She overflowed with enthusiasm about the joy she feels while sitting on a bench and watching the gardeners at work. "You can feel the energy from both the plants and the caretakers," said Alice. "This garden is the creation of loving hands. In spring, at tulip time, it looks like a French impressionist's painting. After an ugly, hectic day, the garden is always an island of beautiful calm. I can't imagine anything more soothing at the end of a crazy eight hours than to stand in this small, intimate patch of green. It is one of the only places I know of where the city smells like the country."

Obviously, experiencing or actively tending an urban garden is not the same as maintaining a garden in suburbia or far out in the countryside where there's always room to swing a hoe or to plant a tree. When I moved to my present home— a second-floor apartment in Southern California—I had no choice but to confine my garden to the tiny balcony that extends off my living room. This space, not much wider than a queen-size bed, has become the focal point for virtually all of my gardening. This is where I snip the aromatic leaves of spices that I add to a meal. This is where I admire a flower as it emerges from a bud. This is where I watch the sun come up and evaporate the dew that forms on the greenery.

Because I travel a great deal, my miniature garden must survive for days or even weeks at a time without attention from me or anyone else. For this reason, I have chosen plants that are strong and forgiving. They are a tough and independent lot, able to go for many days without water or fertilizer. Yet as soon as I return, I invariably put down my suitcase and step outside to see how my plants have fared during my absence. I feel as though I'm being greeted by a happy contingent of my oldest and dearest friends. Despite their outward stoicism, my cacti, succulents, and spices are softies at heart. I guess I am too.

In the course of visiting other urban gardeners around the country, I've discovered that we don't need much space in order to commune with nature. A balcony, a fire escape, or even a shelf next to a window is sufficient. For any of us who choose to make minimal effort, a little soil and a sunny spot go a long way in connecting us to the miracles of nature that keep our planet so wonderfully green and alive.

"I'm a patio gardener just like you," Iris smiled, as we settled into a pair of canary-yellow canvas chairs on the sun-splashed patio of her condominium. "All of my plants grow in pots. But I always tell everybody that as long as I can plunge my hands into some dirt, that's enough for me."

I took a sip of my iced tea and asked Iris why it is so important for her to feel the earth with her fingers, since many gardeners cover their hands when they dig into the soil.

"Y'know," Iris confided, "I've never been able to garden with gloves on. I have a feeling that when my hands are in the ground there is some kind of important communication between me—and the essence of who I am—and my plants. I feel, quite literally, grounded by this touching of the material that my plants grow in.

"Even if it's in a pot," Iris continued, "a plant gives us more than we can ever know. Outside of the fact that it creates oxygen and all the other healthy things that science has documented, a plant is nurturing. When I tend my garden, the plants calm me. That's why I know that people are a lot like plants. In both instances, when you nurture them and give them positive energy, they give you fantastic feedback and become a crucial part of your life. A garden is very good for one's soul, and too many things in today's society are not."

As we talked, it became obvious that Iris maintains a powerful spiritual link with the colorful variety of healthy plants that spill out of her pots. Her collection of poppies, roses, daisies, and other bright flowers seemed to vibrate with positive energy. I felt that same kind of energy emanating from my host.

"I don't see how anybody could plant a seed in the ground and be an atheist," said Iris. "I mean, how does a seed know if it's a tomato or a peony? Yet it always grows into what it's supposed to be. If you ask me, that's an amazing miracle."

Iris has had a lifelong passion for gardening, encouraged by family members who have supported her fascination with flowers from the very beginning.

"When I was little girl growing up in northern Wisconsin, I went to the seed rack at the feed store and found a package of flowers with a name that I couldn't pronounce. It was mignonette, a French flower. I loved the name. It was the most beautiful thing I'd ever heard, and I knew the flowers had to look as good as the name sounded. So I took the package home, made a plot, and I planted my little seeds. I couldn't believe it when one day something actually came up. That was one of the most thrilling events in my young life. The plants grew up and one day I had little flowers. I could never get over that, and I think that has stayed with me for the rest of my life. It's the wonderment of growing things that continues to thrill me. I'm sure that's why gardens have rewarded me all of my days."

Iris concurred with something I've always felt: that any

connection we make to nature's cycles helps us to better understand the essential elements of our humanity, as well as our place in the intricate web of life that spans this planet.

"When I see people in the nursery," Iris said, "there is a relaxed look on their faces that I don't see anywhere else, except maybe in a church or in a museum. It's because the people in the nursery are absorbed in something outside of themselves, and that's very important for one's health.

"In gardening, every day becomes much more of a fulfillment. No matter how old you are, everyone has the strength to nurture a little rosemary bush or an aloe vera plant. And nurturing another living thing always makes you feel better. That's why I think everybody should at least have a few potted plants. As you get older, there is no longer that much time. I'm in my eighties now and every day is precious. There are no more long-distance goals; there's only now, this particular day. Tomorrow may not get here, but today you can have a plant or flower that brings joy into your life."

I met another "pot-bound" gardener during a visit to Minnesota, the state I grew up in and where several members of my family still live. Minnesota is a challenging place to tend plants, and as Rebecca has grown older she has downsized her garden to a patio collection that's smaller than Iris's but bigger than mine. I was admiring her deep-purple salvia as we compared notes on our shared passion.

"Some people think, *I need a lot of money to garden. I need a lot of land. I need a lot of things,*" said Rebecca. "Well, you don't need those things at all. Just take one little pot and plant your first flower. To me, if someone is tending a single pot of flowers on a balcony or the front steps, that's still gardening. Whatever it takes for you to do it, you can make a garden happen. And if that garden helps you feel better about yourself and you feel creative, then you're automatically feeding your soul. A huge bonus is that the positive results of your gardening are immediate."

Gratification can be as close as a trip to your neighborhood nursery or garden center, where millions of showy annuals are sold across the country each year.

"I just turned fifty a few weeks ago," a self-confident gardener named Kate told me. "On my birthday, I bought a huge outdoor pot and filled it with pansies and impatiens. It's not huge, but it's something. Now I like to sit outside and simply be with my itty-bitty garden. I pay attention to what makes me smile, and some flowers make me smile. I'm sure this is why I deliberately chose pansies and impatiens.

"My garden stimulates me in a tactile way, in a visual way," Kate continued. "It also gives me solitude, a quiet balance in my life. When I sit next to my potted plants, I feel like I'm in touch with eternity, with something that goes on and on. I really love that feeling of being fundamentally connected to the cycles of life and of nature."

Kate expressed a sentiment that I've often felt as I stroll through a garden or sit on my balcony and breathe the fresh fragrance of my plants. She said that gardening has brought her a deep and abiding appreciation of all things in nature, including aphids and spider mites! The cycles and rhythms of the natural world are familiar to Kate now, and she feels them oscillating through her own life.

"There's something about accepting the mortality of an exquisitely beautiful plant that has been healthy for me," she explained. "Watching death take place in the garden has helped me grow inside. My spirituality has shifted to include a broader sense of the universe, so now when I'm with nature I have a sense of it being a part of me. I now accept that all things in nature—including me—have their own special functions."

The therapeutic benefits of urban gardening have become well documented in recent years. The August 1997 issue of the *Mind/Body Health Newsletter* concluded that if you work or live in a place that merely offers a window with a view of nature, you ought to consider yourself fortunate. "Overall job satisfaction appears to be significantly higher among [urban] workers with a view of nature," the newsletter reported. "A major survey found that those able to look out on nature scenes also report significantly fewer symptoms and medical ailments than their viewless co-workers. The study went on to suggest that a view of nature from one's hospital window can contribute more to recovery from surgery than many drugs."

Many of us city dwellers need only reflect on our own experiences to know that an hour in the garden can sometimes accomplish more than a comparable interval spent with a skilled psychiatrist.

"Gardening is therapy," Bonnie told me, as we relaxed next to the gurgling fountain in the backyard of her suburban Los Angeles home. "You can't be anxious, you can't be tense, you can't be in a funk. Gardening hearkens back to playing in the sandbox or making mud pies; you just get into it. You're happy, you're giving life to something. A garden is simply wonderful."

"For me," Bonnie confessed, "one of the most compelling attractions of a garden is the sheer simplicity of it. It's something so gorgeous. It's about beauty and simplicity, that's all. I love being able to go out, clip a rose, put it in a vase, and then be able to look at it for a few days. There's something uncomplicated about that; you take joy from it right away. It doesn't matter whether you're rich or poor, whether you live in a big house or an itsy-bitsy apartment; the joyous feeling will be the same.

"In fact, I can't conceive of a person observing a beautiful garden and not being somehow moved or touched. I know that I immediately begin to unwind in a garden. My internal clock slows down. I think gardens probably have that effect on everybody, whether they are conscious of the change or not and whether they're gardeners or not. That's part of what's so magical about a garden."

Another joy of gardening in the present era is the fact that many cities have set aside vacant lots for the use of gardeners. This is a boon to people who live in high-rise apartments or houses that have no place for residents to cultivate an outdoor garden. Some cities not only provide water and fences for their public gardens but also free topsoil, compost, mulch, and other materials. The results of such initiatives can transform an urban community in unexpected ways.

Edie Keen is a professional landscape designer who works part-time for New York City's Parks Department. She's the person in charge of laying out new community gardens for

Operation Green Thumb, an extraordinary program that has created almost eight hundred community gardens on fifteen hundred acres of empty land owned by the city. Once strewn with abandoned cars and garbage, these empty lots now sprout flowers and herbs, vegetables and fruit trees, grass and hedges. These lush plots are tended by thousands of volunteer neighborhood gardeners.

I interviewed Edie at a movie theater, where an independent filmmaker was screening a documentary he had made about New York's community gardens and the thousands of volunteer gardeners who tend them. I was astonished by the tremendous diversity of these gardens, a string of green oases that dot the city from Harlem to the Bowery. Some were odd-shaped lots tightly wedged between tall buildings, while others were ensconced in parklike settings that feel open and spacious. In some gardens, vegetable and flower plots were carefully separated, while in others, the gardeners were given free rein to mix plants as they see fit. Some were as lush and flamboyant as the jungle; others looked tight and tidy. What they all had in common, however, was the pride and support of the neighbors who loved and surrounded them.

"These city-funded gardens make such a positive difference in people's lives," said Edie, who makes a site plan based on what local residents want and how big their lots are. "When you live next to an unauthorized garbage dump full of toxic wastes and moldy mattresses and so forth, it quickly becomes intolerable. People finally get fed up and say, 'I don't want to live this way.'

"After the garden is planted, the first thing to go is the drug dealer. Drug dealers thrive on ugly, dirty places, and they move out when flowers move in. The next thing that happens is more and more people from the community come around and begin to plant and enjoy the new garden. Then you start seeing window boxes full of blossoms on the sides of nearby buildings. The changes are subtle at first but quickly become very obvious."

Edie believes that gardening and beautification are contagious. Once people begin feeling that they can really change their environment for the better, their relationship to their community also changes.

"Older people, who may have hardly left their apartments for years, can finally come outside and find a safe place to sit," Edie told me. "Children wander into the gardens to play. Teachers from nearby schools start bringing students over to start their own plots, and parents come to help them. Eventually, you start seeing the whole community come together around their new gardens, getting to know their neighbors and forming wonderful friendships."

Edie pointed out that gardening is an international language that crosses boundaries between races, creeds, and cultures. Besides raising healthy, fresh, and oftentimes organic produce, urban plots may include vegetables from faraway homelands.

"Some of these items can't easily be found in the grocery stores of New York City, if at all. The gardeners share what they harvest with one another and exchange recipes for their favorite foods. The neighborhood gains a new sense of pride in its diversity.

"An urban garden also has great healing power," said Edie. "Many people who are filled with sorrow have been helped through their grief by spending time among the greenery and flowers. One neighborhood named its community garden after a young man who was shot and killed while building a fence for that same plot of land. This helped the people who live in the area come together and heal the wounds caused by this tragic and violent incident."

In my experience, any kind of garden really softens the sharp corners of a hard-edged landscape. An urban garden puts people in tune with nature. It changes the way their world looks and the way they look at their world.

"A community garden in a big city makes a neighborhood more beautiful and improves property values," Edie emphasized. "Such a garden shows that it's possible to have some impact on how you live, that you can take charge of your life by taking control of a small piece of land. It is positive in every single way that I can think of. The bottom line is that the more community gardens we have, the better off our society will be."

After hearing Edie's inspiring words, I was eager to meet some of the gardeners she was talking about. The next afternoon I went to visit one of the New York City gardens. Nothing could have prepared me for the surprise I felt when my taxi crossed an intersection shadowed by grimy brick tenement buildings and pulled up at an island of greenery that literally teemed with life. In two minutes, I saw more butterflies, honeybees, and birds than I ever imagined existed on Manhattan Island. These creatures probably viewed the garden as a giant salad bar overflowing with flowers, vines, shrubs, vegetables, and even fruit trees. Several acres of vacant land had been subdivided into more than a hundred small plots, each with a unique combination of plants that reflected the personality of its gardener. The gardeners themselves reflected the amazing diversity of the neighborhood: they were young, old, and in-between and seemed to represent every ethnic and racial combination imaginable. When I began interviewing the gardeners, I learned that they hailed from all walks of life and were drawn to the community garden by an equally wide variety of motivations.

"I moved into this neighborhood two months ago," explained Steve, a baby boomer architect who was carefully examining his tomatoes as we talked. "Working here seemed like a good way to get to know my neighbors better. I also find that gardening is very relaxing. I can simply concentrate on tending the plants and forget about my problems and the difficulties going on in the rest of the world. Troubles seem to float away when I'm out here."

Like many gardeners, Steve enjoys the immediacy of a garden's rewards: its aesthetic beauty and daily change, which is sometimes very dramatic. Other benefits are more subtle and less obvious.

"The garden helps me find out who I am and what's important to me," he said. "It provides unconditional love and response, much as a pet or a child does. I also find the garden to be very democratic. Acceptance here is not based upon social position or what kind of car you drive or how much money you have; it's just about being a good person."

A self-described competitive person, Steve told me that he'd learned to become more humble through his experiences in the garden. Unlike architecture, gardening is something Steve knows little about, and he's the first to admit that his abilities are not everything he'd like them to be. It felt awkward at first to be asking questions of the more experienced gardeners around him. Yet Steve has learned to work within his realm of limited knowledge, and he no longer regards gardening as some kind of contest.

"People are put on more of an equal footing in the garden," he pointed out. "Most of the folks here, it doesn't matter what they do for a living. What matters is how they interact with each other. It's more who you are in the garden, not what you do. It's a different kind of community than the one that usually exists in the world of work."

By this time our conversation had attracted the attention of a gardener in the plot adjacent to Steve's, a tanned fellow with jet-black hair and a slender physique. Javier introduced himself as a cabinetmaker, carpenter, and artist who came to New York City sixteen years ago from his native Ecuador. During the summer, he spends much of his free time tending a plot next to Steve's in the same neighborhood garden.

"For me, the garden takes me back to when I was a kid," said Javier, after Steve and I invited him to pull up his lawn chair and join in our discussion. "My grandmother had a wonderful garden when I was child. Gardening seems to come naturally to me; I've always loved growing and tending plants. I started growing cacti when I was only about ten years old."

Javier surprised me when he conceded that his main

motivation for joining the community garden was to get away from people.

"But once I got involved, I met people I liked, and now I really enjoy their company. Still, the main thing for me is working with the plants and admiring their beauty.

"Contact with nature brings about an amazing feeling. I think it's a need that everybody has in their subconscious. Being in touch with nature is a need that is always there, whether people realize it or not. When they do finally make that inner contact with plants, it's as if they've awakened to something long dormant inside them, something that feels very much at home."

According to Javier, gardening also removes some of the craziness of being in a big city. "It gives you a chance to express your creativity, and I firmly believe that all people are creative in their own ways. A lot of times it's very satisfying for me to feel tired at the end of a day of working in the garden, with dirt under my fingernails. I have a great feeling of accomplishment. From time to time, I just come and sit in a chair in my garden, I admire the plants and the way the light hits them. Because of the community garden, I can really appreciate what is beautiful about this neighborhood, about this place that I now call home."

The passion that Steve and Javier feel about their garden plots is shared by thousands of New Yorkers. A 1997 protest at the Pacific Street–Flatbush Avenue community garden over its proposed razing resulted in an agreement with the city in which more than half of the garden would be preserved. Among other things, the protesters tied four thousand gold, blue, green, and crimson ribbons to the chain-link fence surrounding the garden, one of 185 in the city that are threatened with development.

Not long after my visit with Edie Keen and the community gardeners of New York, I flew back to Los Angeles. The next day, I grew curious about an unusually green and luxuriant plot of land that I'd noticed under cultivation along a busy thoroughfare near my apartment. When I went exploring, it turned out to be a community garden much like those created by Operation Green Thumb. The lush, green patch was soothing to the eye, and a surprising number of people were hard at work on a Saturday morning. In a city known for its drive-through car culture, this place was thriving and vibrant. I stopped to talk to a woman with a spurting hose held between her hands, a floppy straw hat perched on her head, and a shy grin playing on her lips.

"My assignment is to water the herb garden," the woman in the straw hat announced. "This is heaven to me. A garden like this is a real oasis. I can't help but smile when I'm here."

"Why do you suppose that's so?" I asked.

"I guess it's because I find a sense of connection and community here that I don't experience anywhere else in my life. I think everybody enjoys gardens, and when it comes right down to it, they're a human necessity."

The herb-waterer's words were echoed a few weeks later by Rucy, an avid gardener whom I interviewed on Mercer Island, Washington. "I can't imagine life without some sort of garden, no matter how tiny," said Rucy. "I believe a garden gives you life. It sustains you when you need to be sustained, and you sustain the garden when it needs to be sustained."

I'm not sure I'd go so far as to say that gardens are essential to every human being's existence, but I would agree that a heartfelt connection with nature—particularly one made during childhood—is a gift that will keep on giving until your dying day. My own childhood was filled with plenty of backyard and vacant-lot adventures: capturing bugs, climbing trees, and skipping rocks across ponds. It disturbs me to speculate that a child growing up today may be denied such pleasures by the relentless encroachment of asphalt and cement on our dwindling open space. I thought about this as I read this bittersweet reflection written by Ann A. Price and published in the March 3, 1996, edition of the *Los Angeles Times*:

> Growing up in the San Fernando Valley as a kid, I cartwheeled barefoot across meadows, slithered up fragrant eucalyptus trunks and hunted pollywogs in the marshy, muddy creek near our tract home.
>
> One summer day, bulldozers thundered through my creek, smoothing its walls for a cement casing. Stepping across the clods of overturned earth, I looked up at the bulldozer driver and asked, "Where did you put the frogs?"
>
> "We moved them," he lied.

Price goes on to point out that, while the "wide open spaces" have all but disappeared from the neighborhoods she had inhabited as a child, nature has not been obliterated: in yards and parkways and other small patches of green—"havens" and "mini-refuges" Price calls them—plants and dirt and bugs and small animals are present to the discerning eye. "It just means you've got to make your own wilderness where you are," Price reminds us.

While Californians continue trying to create havens for plants and animals in their yards and park lands, not everyone enjoys the luxury of owning even a tiny parcel of land. That's why so many people who live in crowded cities are now making an enormous investment of time and energy in their community gardens that I believe serve much the same purpose. These projects are especially important if the younger generation of city dwellers is to have any chance of growing up with an appreciation of the deeper rewards and character-building lessons of gardening.

"The urban community garden is a place where children can learn to nurture and to be patient as they see their way through a long and sometimes complicated project," Sandy Tanck, a Minneapolis urban-gardening teacher, told me during a tour of one of that city's community gardens. "These are very important lessons in a culture that has too much immediate gratification. Gardening can be an extremely creative activity as well. In a garden, children can become artists as well as problem solvers."

I saw the results of Sandy's work in action. Several adult mentors were helping their young charges thin vegetable beds and sow seeds. Sarah, a thirty-something volunteer, was urging a girl named Erica to eat a handful of nasturtium petals. They both swallowed a few and laughed at the sharp, peppery taste. Tim, a mentor with the long limbs of a beanpole, was joined by eleven-year-old Marcos in a quest for the earth-worms that squirmed at the bottom of the compost pile.

"I like to talk to my sunflowers," eight-year-old Amelia Mohammed told me as she squirted the tall plants with a hose. "I tell 'em, 'Grow! Get big! Reach for the sun!' That's why they call 'em sunflowers.

"The plants tell me to grow too. They've taught me that everything grows, including people. I used to be small, like a radish. Now I'm big, like a zucchini. It feels nice to be proud of my plants; it makes me feel strong, like I'll last forever. It's almost like being an Energizer battery."

A few months later, I was in Manhattan again and spent part of a morning in conversation with Ken Druse, a widely published garden designer and writer. A passionate supporter of the kind of community gardens I'd visited in New York and Minneapolis, Druse said that one of the most exciting things about such enterprises is that each is a world unto itself, reflecting the character of the people and places that sur-round it.

"These kinds of gardens infuse real life into neighborhoods, and they show that people truly care about their urban envi-ronment," noted Druse, whose books include *New York City Gardener,* a handbook for urban gardeners in the East's largest city. "I think part of the reason for their popularity is a reac-tion to the American struggle to find peace in a world that is very chaotic. You can find peace in the garden. Gardening represents hope and anticipation for many people. It keeps them going in a way nothing else does."

Druse related the poignant story of a Milwaukee woman

who had been a prominent practitioner of an increasingly popular style of gardening in which an effort is made to use native plants to recreate a landscape that closely resembles a region's natural environment. Living in the Midwest, her specialty was the design of prairie-type gardens, full of indigenous grasses, wildflowers, and low shrubs. Suddenly, she was stricken with a virulent and terminal form of cancer that confined her to her bed. The diagnosis was grim: she was not expected to live longer than a few months.

"The woman lived on a very busy street and didn't have much of a yard," Druse told me. "So her friends got together and created a berm—a low mound of soil—to block the noise and the visual pollution of the street. They covered it with native flowering plants to make a gorgeous buffer. It was beautiful and quickly filled with birds and butterflies and color and fragrance. She did not survive very long, but her last days on Earth were surely made easier by this loving gesture of her gardening friends.

"I can relate to her story because I've learned a lot of life lessons from the garden," Druse continued, in a reverent tone. "I've learned that everything is immortal and, paradoxically, that nothing is immortal. Humans die, and yet everything lives forever, including people. Life is just one long circle, one long chain, that goes on forever with no beginning and no end. I am only here for a short time, and then I will become part of that circle and chain as well. It's like a Möbius strip, a conundrum. When it comes down to it, we're all simply along for the ride."

Philosophical musings about the meaning of life may not

be what you would expect from someone who writes about gardening for a living, yet who better to discuss this topic than a person who is an intimate, daily observer of living things? Gardens are like that. They may start out as simple diversions or practical landscapes confined to a communal plot or a corner of the balcony, and then take over a much larger space in our lives—and our hearts. My own mini-garden has expanded across my deck to the point where I barely have enough room for a single chair in its farthest corner, the place where I like to meditate in the early morning sun.

Many gardeners I've talked to describe laughingly how their "little hobby" grew like Topsy into something bigger—and more meaningful—than they'd ever envisioned. These gardeners express genuine surprise at the way in which plants can gradually take over. My daughter, Nancy, who is blessed with the proverbial green thumb, is slowly—and unintentionally—replacing her lawn with one rosebush after another. At last count she was up to thirty! Another classic example of this phenomenon is the experience of John, the middle-aged Twin Cities reporter whom you met in the previous chapter.

"My garden started four years ago with a little patch of herbs," John recalled in the course of our conversation. "It soon grew to encompass the entire south side of my apartment building near downtown Minneapolis. Now my garden gets substantially bigger every year."

I asked John how this had happened and he launched into a detailed and moving story that reminded me how special a garden can be, how it can become a sacred space in an urban environment that might otherwise provide few places to embrace silence and solitude.

"The garden has been my solution for two problems," John said. "One was filling a fifteen-foot-wide strip that runs along one side of my home, and the other was getting on with my life after the terminal illnesses and subsequent deaths of both of my parents.

"Dad liked to be outside all the time and part of that meant tending to his gardens. Like many kids, I was not much interested in what my folks were doing. So it came as a complete surprise to me in midlife—not long before his death and in much the same way that he had—to find myself completely overtaken by the spirit of working the land.

"When I started gardening, one of the first things that I did was ask my father to help me plant four hundred bulbs that I bought when I'd traveled with my parents and sister to the Netherlands. We planted bulbs from the gardens that we'd seen together, and the next spring, as those tulips were coming up, Dad was in the hospital dying of cancer. Suddenly those green shoots and flowers had a poignant significance that I never expected when we had planted them together the autumn before. The year that Dad died, the tulips were splendid—absolutely magnificent. There was some kind of a triumph in those flowers, in seeing how the cycles of life are repeated in nature.

"Shortly after my father's death, my mother—to whom he had been married for fifty-three years—was tragically stricken with a recurrence of her own cancer. As one of my mother's main caregivers, I wanted to get her yard into better shape because I knew how much pleasure her yard gave her. It had not been well tended, so I planted tulips, peonies, and lilies for her to enjoy. She was very, very ill the following spring and stayed at home, in hospice care. Mom told me she felt so lucky to see the new plants come up, their first tiny shoots breaking through the cold ground. For her, there was some kind of promise in that. For me, the sight of the delicate buds made me think that in such small things, there are often big consolations.

"Gardening and flowers helped get me through the painful time that my sister and I cared for my mother during her illness and helped me after her death. Working in the garden was very consoling. It helped tremendously in dealing with my grief. As I tended to the plants and the earth, I got in touch with so many new feelings in myself.

"It makes me happy to know that somehow the same love of nature that was part of my parents' lives is now an integral part of mine. I like the fact that, despite our many differences in personality and experience, I am now giving something back to the natural world, just as they did."

Of course, the healing power of the urban garden can transform relationships among family members who are still alive, mending emotional fractures and closing psychological rifts that may have caused years of pain. I find that the companionship of a stroll through a city park or some shared gardening chores can often heal minor familial wounds before they begin to deepen and fester. For example, I have always felt better after taking some "nature time" with one of my children or grandchildren if I sense that something is amiss between us. Along the way, we usually find ourselves marveling at a spectacular flower blossom or stopping to admire a colorful bird. By the time we get back to the family member's house or my apartment, neither of us can remember the source of the original tension between us—and we have no interest in finding that source. The wonders of nature—which appear even more miraculous against the backdrop of a city—allow us to let go of the discord and embrace loving feelings once again.

Lee May spent many years as a reporter for the Washington bureau of the *Los Angeles Times* before his semiretirement to one of Atlanta's elegant turn-of-the-century neighborhoods. He lives on a quiet street lined with old red-brick houses, each fronted with sturdy fences, metal flagpoles, brick walkways, and antique street lights. The greenest yard in the district belongs to Lee, now an author and part-time garden columnist for the *The Atlanta Journal-Constitution.*

"When I arrived, it was just an empty canvas," Lee told a visiting reporter from the *San Francisco Examiner.* "I garden twelve months of the year," he added, by way of explaining the explosion of foliage that surrounds his modest home.

Lee can talk your ear off about magnolias, bamboo, creeping thyme, and Carolina jessamine, but what really excites him is recounting the way gardening ended the icy estrangement between Lee and his father, whom he hadn't seen in thirty-nine years. Neither could remember the source of the enmity, but the distance between them had grown wider as the reporter became preoccupied with covering politics in the nation's capital. Through his entire working life, Lee never found time to return to the farm outside Meridian,

Georgia, where he had grown up. Finally, a few years after Lee left the *Times,* the two men agreed to meet.

"I drove up to the house and [Dad] was sitting on the porch, wearing bib overalls and a [baseball] cap," Lee recalled. "No, we didn't hug. We sat on the porch and talked about the weather, about the crops; we soon discovered we had this common bond: gardening."

Lee's father was a lifelong farmer and talked easily about growing peanuts, melons, beans, and corn. In sharp contrast, his son's garden boasted Japanese black pine, cilantro, and Mondo grass. When Lee talked about the care he'd lavished on these nonedible, exotic plants, the old man shook his head, chuckled, and walked away.

"Oh, it was a moment," Lee smiled, but it passed. "Yes, he's growing food and I'm not, but we are still connected to the earth, to each other, this way. Later [Dad] gave me a little box of corn kernels, okra seeds, and peanuts. Of course I planted them." After another visit to his father's farm, Lee brought back a rusted metal bucket that is now nestled between the tomatoes and black bamboo. Asked if the farm bucket makes a handsome match to the elegant Japanese stone lantern that sits nearby, Lee stroked his chin and pondered the question.

"I'd like to think so," he replied at last, a twinkle in his eye.

Stories like John's and Lee's infuse me with hope. Mine is an earnest conviction that an emerging social force will offset the patterns of today's dominant Western-urban culture and eventually lead to a breakdown in the existing barriers between people and nature, even in the harsh human-made environments of high-rise offices, shopping centers, and apartment complexes. I believe that this is particularly important as our technological society continues to advance and specialize, further insulating and distancing us from our natural environment. As we sit in our curtained living rooms, air-conditioned cars, and windowless cubicles, we are almost completely estranged from the instincts and impulses of nature. Instead of wiggling our toes in the grass and smelling the roses, we move in the domain of arbitrary human rules, habits, and restrictions. More often than not, these worlds are at odds with each other, if not on a head-on collision course. With nature so completely shut out of our citified lives, gardening may be our last hope for working out the tensions and contradictions between the natural and human-made environments. Can one garden make a difference? Yes, as a microcosm of our world, I believe it can—and it must.

Writer Richard Reinber summed up the potential consequences of our nature-deprived urban environment in the July/August 1997 issue of *Intuition* magazine:

> We may talk to two dozen people in a given day by fax, e-mail, or phone. Meanwhile, we may not have touched another human hand, much less heard a songbird, smelled a flower, or tasted a fresh radish. In the garden, we meet nature face-to-face, use all of our senses, all of our physical and spiritual muscles. We open ourselves to the unpredictable and make ourselves available to life.
>
> Our deepest yearning is not only for a beautiful place for healing and meditation, but for a better

world for the generations to come. Gardening can help with that. [Urban gardening can] be a way of doing something immediate and effective to help realize our desire for a healthy, sane world for our children.

The challenge that Reinber and other "garden philosophers" presents to us is how we can best integrate urban gardening into the appropriate balance of body-mind-spirit, and how to most effectively turn this activity into an ongoing spiritual practice that nurtures not only our home city and planet, but our souls as well.

# CHAPTER THREE

# Healing in the Garden

My cares and worries seem to melt away when I'm gardening; it is so calming for me. I'm a totally changed person after a day in my garden.

—Mary Jo, a gardener in Iowa

A garden offers us many gifts. Among many other things, it freely provides great beauty, tranquillity, a refuge for wildlife, delicious food, and a place to express our unique creativity. Gardens also provide a safe haven in which to heal and renew ourselves, as well as an environment in which we can experience the wildness and daily miracles of nature. In a garden, we can restore our inner harmony and balance as we gain some measure of control over our lives.

My garden has helped me get through difficult circumstances on many occasions. It has sustained me through a divorce, nurtured me after surgery, eased my stress during times of devastating disappointment, and sustained me through depression and grief. The garden's value is not limited to times of stress and turmoil, however. My garden has enhanced my enjoyment of life on a daily basis, making happy times even more pleasurable.

I've watched with quiet pride as my plants have grown tall and strong, their tiny buds unfolding into bright, beaming flowers. When I see my garden flourish, I regain my resilience, my balanced perspective, and my peace of mind. The garden has proven itself as my best medicine, my partner in recovery and restoration. Through gardening, I can always find my way back into a healthy resonance and a satisfying harmony with the world. And this has been the experience of many other people I've interviewed.

"Even to go sit in the garden is healing," a man in his eighties told me one fine spring day as we shared a park bench and admired a bed full of flowers. "Being in a place like this teaches you who you are. In a garden, your connection to the living energy and spirit of the world is very, very strong."

A nongardener with whom I began a conversation in a Minneapolis public garden was eager to tell me how "enormously therapeutic" it is for her to sit beneath tall trees and admire the garden's great diversity of plants.

"I don't grow anything," she shrugged. "I simply enjoy visiting this garden, particularly when the peonies are opening.

The flowers speak to me in a silent way. I don't reply to them, but I certainly hear them. A garden is a peaceful, calming, and relaxing place; a spiritual refuge that brings me a soothing inner peace."

My own feeling is that our experience of the natural world of the garden helps us reclaim the links to plants and animals that nurture us. As William Shakespeare put it, "Nature teaches beasts to know their friends." And the garden proves itself to be our friend time and time again, though we have a tendency to take this sturdy relationship for granted.

When unexpected illness or unfortunate circumstance separates garden-lovers from their beloved outdoors, they feel a profound and painful loss. This was never more clear to me than during an interview with poet and writer May Sarton a few years before her death. I sat in the living room of her home on the Maine coast while Sarton talked about the aftereffects of a debilitating stroke that had kept her away from her extensive and much-loved garden for many months.

"Not being able to dig in the earth last year was very hard psychologically," Sarton told me. "I lost something—some psychic strength—because I wasn't close to the earth anymore."

Sarton's sense of loss is similar to sentiments I have heard from other gardeners over the years. But I've been blessed with many expressions of joy and comfort as well. These experiences have led me to conclude that there are virtually no traumas in life that can't be eased by touching nature in some way. My personal experience and research on the subject has supported this view, which I find is now widely accepted by gardeners in diverse circumstances and locations. Although they love gardening in all seasons of their emotions, many gardeners seem to unconsciously gravitate toward their plants during times of undue stress or tension. For example, I learned a great deal about the therapeutic value of gardening during the course of interviewing Kate, a woman in her late forties who is one of many middle-aged children dealing with aging parents.

"Not long ago," she told me, "I gave my father and step-mother a big terra-cotta pot of geraniums. They were both really feeling down in the dumps, and I thought that caring for a plant might help ease their depression. I knew that buying living, flowering plants was something that they would never do for themselves."

Kate was prompted to present her parents with this gift after buying and planting a pot of geraniums of her own a few months earlier.

"I don't have children and planting those flowers brought out the maternal, nurturing part of me. I felt better instantly. And you know what the best surprise has been? Since I've given a pot of geraniums to my parents, they tell me how those plants are doing every single time we talk. Their whole outlook on life has changed."

Having something as simple, yet vital, as a plant to take care of can make all the difference to people whose homes are devoid of any living thing besides themselves. The life force that flows through every plant and animal has a power that reaches out to us on an unconscious level. We find ourselves a partner in nature's intricate web when we allow even an infinitesimal amount of that life-force energy to flow from the garden into ourselves.

Kate's story about the pot of geraniums and its impact on her elderly parents reminded me of a remarkable couple whom I met in upstate New York where they helped create one of the country's "greenest" nursing homes.

Acting on his passionate faith in the garden's life-force connection has transformed Dr. Bill Thomas into a physician with a mission. He and his wife, Judy, want every nursing home in America to be a place that hums with positive energy. Their vision is of residents with a sense of purpose, vitality, and community rather than the usual predictability, boredom, and loneliness.

Bill and Judy have developed something they call The Eden Alternative, an approach that succeeds at helping nursing homes become not only more livable but also more life affirming. One of the most important tenets of their philosophy is that people are happier and healthier when they are surrounded by healthy living plants. Acting on this conviction, they began their project by placing thousands of plants in the eighty-bed nursing home where Bill was then serving as medical director. The positive therapeutic results that followed manifest the life-embracing philosophy Bill and Judy espouse in their continuing work today with both children and the elderly. As a direct result of their success, variations on The Eden Alternative philosophy have been implemented at many nursing homes around the country.

"I was really lucky to grow up in a rural area," Bill

informed me as we sat beneath a vine-draped arbor on the grounds of the hilltop home he shares with Judy. Bill recalled that his extended family of aunts and uncles, grandparents and great-grandparents had always lived in close proximity to the small New York farm where he was raised. "We had pigs, cows, and a garden—not because it was a fun hobby but because we put up food to be eaten. Since we had very little money, it was what we needed in order to get by."

Young Bill was very strongly affected by this rural lifestyle and grew up dreaming that he'd recreate that kind of existence for himself someday.

"I wound up going to Harvard Medical School where they are really clear about what constitutes achievement. By the time I became a doctor and started working at a nursing home, I had two competing viewpoints within me: one that regarded older people as important and valuable, the other that labeled them as worthless and no fun. I finally resolved this conflict by recognizing that modern medicine was not addressing the latent spirit of folks in nursing homes, which in turn affected my attitudes toward what I wanted to offer to these people."

I asked Bill how gardening relates to the well-being of nursing home patients.

"To take care of somebody is to help that person grow, just as you nurture a garden in order to help it grow. A good gardener takes care of the soil and the soil takes care of the plant. When you nurture an individual, as with a plant, you make that person stronger and better able to resist disease. This is where we've gotten off the track in medicine. Physicians let the 'soil' that is our society decay and treat the result of that neglect with drugs and operations. My philosophy is that a physician has an obligation to look at society and try to rejuvenate and enrich it, which will make medical treatment less necessary.

"I started implementing my ideas after concluding that people in nursing homes were stuck. On their own, they couldn't create an environment that was enlivened. The Eden Alternative began with the notion that nursing homes are horrible places that are bad for the human spirit. We found terrible loneliness caused by a lack of companionship, a lack of opportunity to give care, and a high incidence of boredom. Every day was the same. We decided to build a healthy natural habitat for these frail, elderly people, an environment where they could thrive as human beings. We wanted an environment where you could not predict what is going to happen next, where there is variety and spontaneity—like real life, not some kind of endless tape loop. You have to believe that every individual is capable of personal growth, and when it comes to nursing homes, that's something a lot of people really don't believe."

Judy and Bill reviewed the growing body of research suggesting that indoor plants have a positive impact on people. A survey by Steven Kaplan of the University of Michigan's environmental psychology department, for example, concludes that the brain seems more aroused and soothed by nature. Other academic studies suggest horticulture therapy may lower blood pressure, slow bone loss, improve circulation, and reduce stress. Still others hint at a vital function of electrical fields within plants, which seem to respond to similar fields in the environment and even within humans. Such conclusions supported the Thomases' own observations from various nursing home experiences.

"We changed the nursing home environment by bringing in a huge number of plants, not just to the lobby but right into people's rooms. Residents were given the opportunity to take care of the plants. Besides potted plants in rooms, we developed outdoor raised-bed gardens for residents, because people are often eager to put their hands in the soil. We got those people confined indoors involved with growing plants from seeds and working with hydroponics.

"Companionship was the next thing we addressed. Human companions are best, but humans also have been doing pretty well for thousands of years with domesticated animals. So we brought in dogs, cats, parrots, parakeets, chickens, rabbits, chinchillas, whatever it took. Our nursing home now has more animals and plants than people."

One measure of the healing power of The Eden Alternative is reflected in raw statistics. The first nursing home for which the Thomases consulted had about 15 percent fewer deaths the first year and 25 percent fewer deaths the second year, when compared to conventional nursing homes. Rates of infection and medical prescription fell by more than half. Bill and Judy are now fully convinced that elderly people who have a plant or animal to care for will live longer and enjoy happier, healthier lives.

"Because nursing homes ordinarily suffer from an over-abundance of people," Bill told me, "we decided to dilute the human factor with animals and plants to create a more diverse environment. Just as a good gardener takes care of his or her soil, the nursing home takes good care of its human habitat because that enriches the lives of residents and improves their overall quality of life.

"If you think about it, people all over the world go to great lengths to put themselves in natural environments. Look at New York's Central Park: people will never build on it because they need this green oasis so badly. If developers ever paved over that park, New Yorkers would be devastated. Parks are a terrific relief valve for an overly humanized environment, but most nursing homes don't offer anything like the connection with nature that a park provides."

In addition to nursing homes, many adult day-care centers are following The Eden Alternative philosophy. The same approach could be implemented in any institution that handles lots of people, including schools, factories, prisons, psychiatric wards, hospices, office buildings, and hospitals. As Bill points out, "There is a huge need for this program because people not only feel disconnected from nature, they feel powerless and helpless with respect to changing their circumstances in every arena of life. When people have plants to care for, they feel nurturing and empowered."

A shift in priorities won't come overnight, Thomas predicted, but rather as part of a gradual evolution of society toward a recognition of the transformative and healing power of nature.

"In her habitats, nature always mixes growth and decay, youth and age," Bill reminded me. I later learned that programs similar to The Eden Alternative are now integrated into nursing homes, adult day-care centers, and retirement communities specializing in the care of individuals suffering from Alzheimer's disease. In Tarboro, North Carolina, for example, the Albemarle retirement center has a large courtyard garden featuring five distinct "sensory zones": tranquillity, water, bird, flower, and vegetable. Such gardens often trigger comforting associations for patients with Alzheimer's disease whose brains tend to favor sensory and physical domains.

Gardening as therapy is not limited to older folks. My friend Jeannie, for example, helps design and carry out the Horticultural Therapy Program at the Minnesota Landscape Arboretum, through which eleven- to fifteen-year-old children and the elderly join forces each summer to tend plants in a section of the arboretum. The project is a great success, partly because it accommodates the age-specific needs of both the young and the elderly. Raised beds are equally accessible to youngsters and people in wheelchairs. Shrubs and flowers are chosen that smell, look, and feel good. There are plenty of shade trees, benches, and drinking fountains, which have special appeal to members of both age groups.

Jeannie stressed that the intergenerational gardening experience was intentionally designed to please all the senses. She was right. Participants are plunged into an aesthetically stimulating environment filled with the heady scents and textures of roses, sunflowers, and daisies, along with more than fifty other species of flowering plants and vegetables.

"Our garden promotes the continued well-being of people

*Tending the Earth, Mending the Spirit*

who are already well and enhances healing among those who may need further healing," Jeannie told me during a walking tour of the arboretum. "We've seen our program succeed in many different ways. People who feel isolated, for example, form partnerships and share with others all the joys and delights of sowing seeds and helping plants grow. Those who don't speak much tend to become more sociable. People who are depressed find their spirits lifting and their moods lightening."

Some of the positive results of the program were unexpected, according to Jeannie, who ticked off a long list of benefits.

"Older gardeners who have memory problems will often recall a great deal through the sights, sounds, smells, and textures of the plants, flowers, and soil. A garden is full of 'memory triggers.' We've also seen a great many positive results in the physical responses of the elderly. Flexibility increases as they weed, prune, and water, with more range of motion in arms, fingers, and legs. The sun and fresh air, of course, does everyone good."

Jeannie's program oversees the planting of new gardens each spring, an activity that gives participants something to get excited about whether they're eight years old or eighty. My friend said the experience has convinced her that when we lose our connectedness with the earth, we become more disconnected from other humans—and ourselves.

"Without our feelings of connectedness to our planet and to each other," she concluded, "I don't see how any of us can ever lead healthy, happy lives—or even begin to solve the world's problems. There's a real value that comes in the healthful nurturing and tending not only of plants but also of people."

Two thousand miles away, in Mill Valley, California, a similar philosophy is espoused by Cris Chater, coordinator of a "do-it-themselves" garden for elderly but active residents of the Redwoods Retirement Center.

"For many people who live here," Chater told the *San Francisco Examiner,* "it's a worrisome thing to move into [a retirement community] and have to give up gardening. . . . But this place has tai-chi and nutrition and art classes, and now it has gardening too."

Chater's garden design incorporates raised beds that can be tended by residents sitting on benches or in wheelchairs, wide and level paths that are easy to negotiate, and plants that are specially chosen to attract birds and butterflies. Vegetable patches are filled with such popular choices as tomatoes, pumpkins, sweet corn, and a dozen varieties of lettuce. The garden at Redwoods has been lined with lavender and roses to provide plenty of fragrance for the visually impaired, along with a tasty spectrum of herbs and spices that residents are encouraged to use in their cooking. Residents vetoed a proposal to install an automatic watering system, insisting that they'd rather water the garden themselves. They also donated old clothes that gardeners used to make several life-size scarecrows.

"I've never seen anything like it," eighty-one-year-old Redwoods resident Anneke Foschler told a reporter from a local newspaper. "It's very uplifting for us to garden and to build something together."

The more I travel, the more often I hear people singing praises to the healing power of nature. Sue Benson, who helps organize community gardens in an inner-city neighborhood, told me that she has never encountered anything human that could transform her—and her clients—the way nature does.

"Gardens help me become stronger, and they heal me when I'm sick," explained Sue. "I've seen this many, many times with myself as well as with others. Trees, shrubs, flowers, and even grass can change and heal us the way other things can't. They turn our world into a wonderful, magical, and beautiful place to be."

Sue's experience among the hard-pressed, low-income residents living at the decaying core of a big city has led her to conclude that "gardening can inspire passion, inspiration, and energy. I definitely believe that a lot of personal transformation can and does occur in this way. For example, gardening can help us get to know our neighbors at a time when most of us not only don't know our neighbors but don't want to know them."

Sue described today's sense of alienation as very unhealthy for society and expressed hope that closer ties to nature will bring human beings closer together.

"I think children are especially affected by the healing, nurturing power of plants without consciously being aware of it," said Sue. "There's some kind of 'soul connection' between kids and plants. They don't analyze it, yet the experience manifests itself in their feeling good and sensing that they are an integral part of the natural world. This is a life lesson from the garden that can change children for the better, and it's one that we adults need to constantly relearn."

As if on cue, an eight-year-old boy appeared before us, his arms loaded with freshly picked zucchini. He had spent the morning working in the same community garden where Sue and I had been talking. After Sue introduced us, I asked Tommy what he enjoyed about gardening.

"I like to help plant seeds, pull weeds, and harvest vegetables," said Tommy. "I like to bring food home from the garden and give it to my mom. But the part I like the very best about gardening is helping other people."

Young Tommy was describing a range of experiences that will probably keep him spending time in various kinds of gardens for the rest of his life. You don't have to be an adult to understand this attraction; the only qualification is to be a human. This metaphysical connection between people and plants is sometimes difficult to describe in words, but it is definitely real—and surprisingly powerful.

In suburban San Francisco, for example, scores of former inmates from the San Bruno Jail have weeded the spinach beds and watered the strawberry patches of the Carroll Street Garden, an innovative project that uses gardening for self-esteem boosting and employment training.

"At first it was like, 'To hell with this, I'm not going to be planting no damn flowers,'" a former inmate named Myron scowled in a 1997 interview with *American Way* magazine reporter Debi Howell. "But after being in the garden itself, I felt secure. . . . I like watching these things grow that I made happen. It makes me feel good."

Another Carroll Street participant—an eighteen-year-old

crack addict—said that when she took a bag of garden-grown veggies home to her grandmother, she received the first bit of praise she can remember ever hearing from a family member.

The Carroll Street Garden is the brainchild of former jail counselor Catherine Sneed, who convinced the local sheriff to allow inmates and parolees to transform a trash-strewn vacant lot into a lush, expansive garden that now supplies produce to such acclaimed Bay Area restaurants as Chez Panisse. A follow-up study of participants in the program found that those involved in the garden were more likely to kick drugs, reintegrate with their families, and dump old crime buddies than those who did not participate. A growing number of former inmates have landed garden-related jobs as a direct result of their experience with Carroll Street. Others have graduated from drug-rehabilitation programs in which they were inspired to enroll after working in the garden.

The results of projects like these support the conclusion of a 1992 study by Virginia Polytechnic University, which found that contact with the natural environment is important to the psychological well-being of adults in five key areas: aesthetics, mental and emotional stimulation, self-expression and personalization, social interaction, and physical health. Other experts have noted that one hour in the garden can reduce a person's blood pressure almost as much as does an hour of meditation, and that violent and antisocial behavior declines among institutionalized individuals who are given an opportunity to garden. Physiologists report greater muscle relaxation, slower breathing, and increased endorphin production among gardeners.

It seems that anyone who spends time in a garden intuitively understands the therapeutic value of tending plants, and all of us who've seen a perfect flower know what joy can come simply from beholding nature's magnificence. Writer Steven H. Davis eloquently articulated this point in an issue of the *Maximizing Human Potential* newsletter:

> The space we call a garden—whether a random grouping of plants surrounding an outdoor residential patio or an expansive, exquisitely landscaped public garden—is a non-threatening place. It's a quiet spot where we can reflect, evaluate, think, cope, and mentally restore ourselves. The garden is also a place where people can let go of their aggressions and redirect their focus and energies for positive purposes.
>
> Always changing, the garden is a stimulating place filled with excitement and discovery. We can see the beautiful blossoms, smell their enticing fragrance, touch their softness, hear their brushing in a gentle breeze and, after their flowering, even taste the fruit that follows. The garden is a place where we can experience quiet contemplation as well as noisy socialization, where encouragement, confidence, self-esteem, creativity, and a sense of accomplishment can flower and flourish. . . .
>
> Because gardens do not discriminate in their response to the gardener, regardless of his or her disabling condition or level of gardening ability, the

benefits associated with gardening can be reaped by anyone who desires them.

One of my interviewees, a middle-aged gardener named Donald, used simpler words to drive home a similar point. According to Donald, there is nothing like twenty minutes in the garden to dispel the darkness of a gloomy or crabby mood.

"I cheer up in the garden," Donald said. "It's so perfect: the balance of plants, earth, breeze, fragrance, and sunlight. Gardening is an internal thing for me, not merely external. It's a spiritual, feeling kind of thing. I guess you might say that the garden has become my best friend."

A Tennessee gardener I met on an earlier trip put it this way: "Gardening is my meditation. Four walls in a house can depress me no end, so that's why you'll find me in the garden during at least some part of every single day."

And this from Jean, another Memphis gardener: "The garden has really helped me deal with my personal losses. It's always a comfort to see the plants come back every year. It's an affirmation that I, too, can get through anything. There's a reassurance that if the plants can hang on, I can hang on too. Their strength is both an inspiration and a reinforcement of the reality that people are part of the natural environment as well. The natural life cycle of plants is like the natural life cycle of human beings—bad things happen to them just as they happen to us—and that keeps me from feeling terribly alone."

There is probably no time when the healing power of a garden is more welcome and soothing than after the death of a loved one. Again and again, people have told me heartrending tales about the crucial role gardening played in their recovery of equilibrium after the passing of someone special.

"My husband died suddenly on my birthday," Evelyn told me, "and I went out and made a garden. Now you must realize that I had never, ever, cultivated a garden in my life. Yet it was my salvation.

"I started digging and planting and tending. Before I knew it, I had put all of my love and all of my sorrow into the earth. The plants got me through my sadness. I'm sure I could not have made it without them. That's how I learned that a garden can heal the spirit."

Death may cause some mourners to start a garden for the first time, losing themselves in the timeless miracles of nature. For others, death spurs a retreat from the garden, to be followed in due course by a reconnection with the earth. Geneva, who was introduced in chapter 1, stopped gardening for two years following her husband's untimely demise. They had spent so many happy hours gardening, she told me, that it was too painful to even look at her flower beds.

"I'm not sure exactly why I left the garden," Geneva confessed. "But now I'm back in it again, with just as much passion. It's a smaller garden this time, but I enjoy it just as much as the big one we used to have. For me, there really is a sense of healing there. Simply being out in my garden helps me feel whole and healthy. That's why sometimes I simply sit down among my flowers. I don't want to go anywhere else, I don't want to do anything else, so I'll sit as long as I like. It's important to relax the mind and the body, and the garden is a place where I can always do exactly that."

Geneva has simplified her life considerably since her husband's death and takes comfort from the simple lessons and enduring truths she learns in her garden.

"I've come to realize," she continued, "how it's possible for me to flourish and to spread joy through my presence in the lives of my loved ones, much like a garden does. When I tend my plants, I can feel myself becoming full of life, and I know now that I need the same kind of nourishment that all growing things need. When my hands are in the dirt and I can see how my plants are thriving on the outside, I can feel myself thriving on the inside too. I'm always being nurtured when I'm connected with the sky, the rain, and the earth."

Geneva's thoughtful comments echoed my own feelings and brought to mind a similar experience of my own. It occurred several years ago, after I attended a week-long spiritual retreat at a remote location in the California desert. For seven days, a small group of us meditated, listened to wise teachers, discussed questions involving human consciousness, and engaged in silent contemplation. As you can imagine, by the end of our time together my companions and I had quieted ourselves to the point where our minds felt like calm forest pools, lacking the usual ripples of distraction and anxiety.

"When you return to the 'real world,'" our seminar leader advised us, "you will be in a highly sensitive state of awareness. You will feel overwhelmed by the sheer volume of sensory input that daily life presents to you. This can be very disorienting and uncomfortable, and your first impulse may be to stay in bed and pull the covers over your head."

I looked at the others, and we all nodded in agreement. The

prospect of rejoining the noisy, crowded world was daunting. None of us knew for certain how we would react.

"Here's my advice," our leader continued. "Take some time to 'ground' yourself, making physical contact with the earth as a way of regaining your equilibrium amid the tumult. It sounds simple, but it works."

Two days later, I was plunged back into the uptight hubbub of Washington, D.C., where I was living at the time. Sure enough, the frenetic energy of the city felt overwhelming and I wasn't sure how to cope. As if by instinct, I slowly walked to the Chesapeake and Ohio canal that runs parallel to the Potomac River, not far from my Georgetown loft. Ignoring the curious stares of the men and women in business suits who swept by me on their lunch hours, I shucked my shoes, closed my eyes, and rooted myself in a grassy spot next to the canal. I felt the cool grass and damp soil beneath my feet. As I wriggled my toes, a knowing smile appeared on my lips. As Geneva might say, I felt connected with the sun, the sky, the water, and the earth. I had never felt so much at home; I felt as "grounded" as the leader of our retreat had predicted.

Gardens work their magic in an infinite number of ways. During an interview in her flower-filled home, my longtime neighbor Merrilyn told me that a eulogist at her husband's funeral recited Robert Frost's poem, "After Apple Picking."

"In this poem, Frost compares the apple harvest of autumn to the dying of a loved one," a teary-eyed Merrilyn recalled. "One line says, 'There's a barrel I didn't fill and there may be a few apples left upon the bough, but I am done with apple picking now.' That verse always brings tears to my eyes, yet it's a wonderful way of thinking about gardening—and about life as a whole."

Everyone seems to have a favorite memory about certain plants, particularly those that were special to them during childhood. I can think of two kinds of flowers, for example, that have always evoked strong emotional responses in me.

When my daughter, Nancy, comes to visit, she never fails to notice the five pots of red geraniums that provide the only splash of color on my apartment's balcony, otherwise crowded with succulents and cacti.

"That was always Grandma's flower," she reminds me, with a knowing smile. "Red geraniums make me think of her."

I had never made the connection consciously until Nancy pointed it out, but it's true. No matter how big or small my mother's garden was, she always managed to save a space for red geraniums. I have been carrying on the tradition without realizing it. There is something very comforting about that.

For special occasions, my mother also had a clear preference among flowers. When circumstance demanded something particularly rare and exquisite, a peach-colored rose was always her favorite. My mom had little use for the traditional pink or red rose. In fact, she never grew roses of any kind, despite a lifelong interest in gardening. Yet she was invariably drawn to the delicate and unusual shades of orange and yellow that are found in certain varieties of the old-fashioned, long-stemmed Peace roses. As an adult, I always knew that I could never go wrong if I presented her with this flower, which always represented the absolute ultimate in beauty for my mother. In the weeks before her death, the peach-colored rose is what I always brought to the hospice, and she remained awestruck by its perfection. At some point during this terrible ordeal, my mom said that she wanted everyone attending her memorial service to be given such a rose, which is exactly what we did. To this day, whenever members of my family get together, at some point someone in the group will mention this lovely and loving gesture. It makes us smile and swells our hearts to remember my mother in this way. Occasionally I'll notice a single, perfect, peach-colored rose in a florist's shop and feel compelled to bring the flower home, where it is given a place of honor. For the next few days, I admire its exceptional beauty and am filled with fond memories of the special woman who nurtured and cared for me.

The inner calm we feel when we have such positive associations is certainly one of the reasons we are so attracted to gardens, particularly those that are adorned with flowers. Many of the gardeners I've interviewed describe the experience of being in their gardens as very "centering" or "grounding." This is especially true if the gardener spends any length of time around his or her favorite plants. These gardeners talk about the distractions, stresses, and scattered energy of their daily lives fading away, in much the same way that static electricity disappears when we touch an earthbound object. It's almost as if we need some direct contact with the soil in order to keep our minds clear, our hearts open, and our spirits light. Through this contact, we are also reminded of our own strength, as environmental activist and writer Edward Abbey once noted in an eloquent passage:

Anything that lives where it would seem that nothing could live, enduring extremes of heat and cold, sunlight and storm, parching aridity and sudden cloudbursts, any such creature, beast, bird, or flower, testifies to the grandeur and heroism inherent in all forms of life. Including the human. Even in us.

By definition, it seems, gardens are quiet and welcoming places where we quickly find refuge in a soothing private space within ourselves. As a happy result, gardens can become a refuge from the incessant noise pollution of the urban world, and from the disturbances and tensions that unwanted sounds produce. Author Sue Minter took this notion a step further in her inspiring book *The Healing Garden: A Natural Haven for Body, Senses and Spirit:*

From the sighing and rustling of leaves and stems in the breeze, to the tinkling or rushing of water, sounds in the garden can trigger vivid memories and can bring to mind happy incidents in the past, often from childhood. These can have a psychologically healing effect, especially against depression, and as an antidote to the strains of everyday pressures and uncertainties.

When we grow into adulthood, our pleasant associations with gardens of the past can sometimes help us make the best of the difficult challenges we face in the present.

"The garden was always my special place to play as a child," a Southern California gardening enthusiast named Diane revealed to me in the course of a thoughtful conversation. "I never would have predicted that it would eventually become my place for solace and healing as an adult. I can vent sorrow and anger and other troubling emotions in my garden, yet I can still find fun there as well."

Although she was not yet sixty when I interviewed her, Diane had already outlived two of her children. The shock of these tragic losses had proven almost more than she could bear. She swears that her garden enabled her to survive and, ultimately, to prevail. Diane shared her story this way:

"When I lost my son to an untimely death, at age eleven, I also lost the whole frontyard. The entire lawn went. I was out there like a madwoman, tearing up the grass. I guess it was a creative, satisfying way to get rid of my hurt and anger and bitterness. It helped resolve those emotions for me.

"Thirteen years later, my daughter died. She was only twenty-seven. The saddest thing about these two events was that I still really wanted to be a mother. I had all this love of mothering still inside me. So what better way to remain a mother than to go into the garden and tend plants? I found that even your tears have value in the garden, because their salt and moisture replenish the earth.

"There's an old Jewish custom that when you bury someone, you don't embalm them and you bury them in a coffin that doesn't have any nails. This allows the body to go back into the earth. Through this ritual, we become bonded with the planet and a part of our universe all over again.

"I've planted an olive tree next to my children's graves, and I hope to have the soil from my own grave mixed with theirs when I die, so that we will have that last physical connection. I'd also like to have ivy planted on our plots, so that the vines and the leaves will mingle above our graves when we are finally together again.

"Gardening is my strength, as were my children, and gardening is my pleasure, as were my children. A garden has seasons, good and bad parts, challenging and easy parts, just as children do. Both your garden and your children always need you. Both love you unconditionally.

"When you lose someone, it's a terrible loss and yet you, as a person, must go on. You rebuild your life by nurturing and growing and being kind to yourself. You see that life is renewed, that there's always reason for optimism. You try something and hope for the best, knowing that you may not get exactly what you want or what you expect. In the same way that children come in and out of our lives, the garden provides plants and flowers and birds that pass through, giving pleasure while they are among us. In all these ways—and many more—the garden has shown its blessings to me."

I've reflected on Diane's story a great deal since she first related it to me. I believe that her total absorption in gardening not only helps Diane deal with some of the deep pain brought on by the deaths of her children but also may have opened Diane to a new level of experience and perception. I found support for this idea during a telephone conversation with drawing teacher Betty Edwards, an avid gardener best known for her book *Drawing on the Right Side of the Brain,* which describes ways in which we can unblock the brain's more creative and intuitive hemisphere.

"Gardening seems to result in a slight shift in consciousness toward the right brain," Edwards confirmed. "You can lose track of time in this state and become very focused on what you're doing. Like meditation or yoga, gardening tends to put people in the moment."

According to Edwards, one result of this phenomenon is that the gardener makes a cognitive shift that is not only pleasurable, but meaningful.

"People gain insights into thoughts and feelings that were hidden from their consciousness before. The rational half of your brain—the left hemisphere—is dampened somewhat, which quiets some of the mind's chatter and allows you to escape ordinary thinking patterns. This is why gardening can expand your awareness and give you the kind of wider range of perception that can help you see things that you didn't see before. Things may seem beautiful that you never before thought of as beautiful. Life seems so much richer in this state, which may partially explain why people love gardening so much."

Based on my own experiences, as well as those of many gardeners I've interviewed, the shift in perspective wrought by the garden often yields unanticipated results. If I've just received a troubling phone call or letter, for example, a stroll through my nearest neighborhood park can offer up the perfect, calming response. If I'm not sure how to reach out to a friend in turmoil or a family member in need, an hour spent puttering among my potted plants may provide the answer. And if I'm just getting over a cold or the flu, there's nothing like an admiring tour of a friend's sun-splashed flower garden to speed the momentum of recovery.

Does a garden hold the power to improve our mental health? Of course it does. One of the finest expressions of this truth appeared in a column by David Rooks that was published by the *Hot Springs Journal* out of South Dakota:

> Every hour in the garden is a homily, a lesson in the logic of languid motion; the voluptuous curve of yellow squash beneath umbrellas of leaves, the drooping sigh of ripe green beans bowing before their picking, tomatoes turning sunburnt red pull branches down to shield them. These teach the tender miracle of the union of soil with seed: Bring love in a pail of water and more abundance than you could ever expect grows well within your reach.
>
> Linger a little longer and the homily becomes a sermon. The mind abandoned of care sometimes dwells on deeper things: like how gardens within their tilling resemble the combined desires of hearts. Like planted seeds, the deeper nature of wishes is more clearly revealed by time. One moment's glance at gentleness blossoms into love, the quick temper of childhood becomes arrogance in the man, a kindness in an airport births grace in a foreign land. Seeds of vanity take in Barbie dolls, seeds of hate in GI Joes, or not—depending upon the individual's soul.

I've learned over the years that the healing power of the plants—be it mental, physical, or spiritual—is a gift that must be shared in order to be fully appreciated. In the act of giving, some of this positive energy always flows back in our direction. The greatest pleasure, however, is in knowing that your offering may profoundly affect another person's life.

Here's an excerpt from another conversation on the theme of inner healing. It involves Doris, a lifelong gardener whom I interviewed during a visit to Nashville, Tennessee.

"After my mother died," Doris began, "one of my dear friends sent to our home a big basket of incredibly beautiful tulips. It brought such a gorgeous light into my life again, at a time when I had lost one of the very brightest spots in my life. I can't begin to tell you how much that helped me heal the open wound of my loss.

"My other anecdote is about Patrick, the twenty-nine-year-old son that my husband Joe and I have. Patrick has Down's syndrome and is a very capable young man. He works bagging groceries in a supermarket. But Patrick has always been very afraid of thunderstorms. I have tried to explain to him over the years that we need to have storms in order to get rain-water. 'When trees and flowers get thirsty,' I've told him, 'they need a drink from the rain.' None of my explanations have ever worked, however.

"This spring, our son came home one day with a seedling that someone had given him. I managed to keep it alive long enough to get it started in the garden. Luckily, it wasn't a delicate plant and it has prospered. I took him outside recently to show him how his little seedling had tripled in size.

"'Look, Patrick,' I said, 'here is that tiny plant that you gave me!'

"He looked at it quietly for a moment, then turned to me and said, 'Yes, Momma, and it has to have rain. It needs to get a drink from the thunderstorms.'

"I smiled, clasped my hands together, and thought to myself, *Thank you, Lord! We don't have to have that discussion ever again. You have cured my son's fear.*"

The healing power that Doris and Patrick discovered in the garden may not have been as dramatic and profound as others have experienced, yet the cumulative effect of seemingly minor miracles adds up. No matter how large or small your garden is, it can provide a sense of safety and comfort. And through a deepening relationship with nature—cultivated through various potted plants, flowers, trees, and vegetables—each of us can gather strength and renew our spirits.

"I have a daisy growing just outside the window of my office," my friend Ilene, a writer and artist based in Venice, California, told me one day. "I try to remember to look up at it every so often when I'm at the computer. That daisy is a reminder of nature, and looking at it has the effect of nourishing me and quieting my mind."

Ilene is not the first gardener I've met who relies on the garden to stay on an even mental keel, as a kind of natural balm to treat the various psychological bruises suffered during the course of a typical day.

"One of the great things about gardening is that it helps you appreciate the 'now,'" I was reminded by Mia Amato, syndicated garden columnist and author of *The Garden*

*Explored.* "Living in the present moment is a great gift, because in the global sense, our lives are very brief and we tend to forget that fact. In the garden, we see evidence of life's fleeting quality every single day. A garden teaches us how to shift our consciousness away from the past and future to more fully appreciate the 'now.' When we do that, we can relax about a lot of things that really don't matter."

During a stint as a garden writer for the *San Francisco Examiner,* Mia was approached by a number of AIDS caregivers who told her that gardening was very therapeutic for them, as well as for the AIDS patients they were taking care of.

"I've talked to people who were dealing with very deep grief who said they wouldn't have made it without their gardens," Mia told me. "Watching flowers open and plants growing is very nurturing for people who have holes in their hearts. And of course, nothing is more satisfying than pulling weeds when you're feeling frustrated or angry."

The transience of life is a truth that we all must accept, and the ephemeral beauty of nature provides a wonderful setting in which to reflect on this reality. The garden as sanctuary for contemplation and restoration is a tradition that prevails in almost every society that has risen above the subsistence level. From the lush Hanging Gardens of Babylon to the austere Zen gardens of Japan, for thousands of years we have used gardens to feed our souls as well as our bodies. There's a Talmudic saying in the Jewish tradition that advises, "Before you go to meet the Messiah, plant your garden."

A garden is a partnership with nature, and the process of creating and maintaining such a special space brings us not only closer to nature but also closer to God, however we choose to define that term. When we create a healing landscape, we give ourselves a piece of heaven on earth that we can step into whenever our souls need soothing. The gift of the garden is indeed a gift of sacred space.

Gardening's healing power is known and appreciated in virtually all human societies, but in the United States the garden's abundant, health-giving energy traditionally has been downplayed, marginalized, or ignored. Yet the stories and documentary evidence I have gathered convince me that we are ignoring one of the strongest and most accessible — not to mention renewable—of all imaginable resources for healthy living. My hope is that we will heed the wisdom of our gardeners and make the world a better place.

## CHAPTER FOUR

# The Language of Flowers

A flower is like a beautiful song that lingers in your
thoughts. If you're sad, it makes you smile and feel a lot
of nice things.

—A gardener in Tennessee

Tom Norris sent seventy-five orchids to a woman he barely
knew. Marianne received his bouquet the day after their very
first date. Tom concedes that it was an extravagant gesture
but never doubted that it was worth every penny.

What was he saying to her?

You already know the answer.

"I was telling Marianne that I was falling in love," Tom

smiled, with a dreamy look in his eyes. "I was declaring to her that no matter how difficult it was to imagine, we were going to spend our lives together: that we would get married."

I asked if Marianne got the message.

"She was floored," said Tom, laughing at the memory. "And, yes, we did fall in love with each other and eventually get married. She felt the same way I did after that date, and we've been together now for thirteen years."

I could tell that this middle-aged man was still head over heels in love with his wife. It didn't surprise me when Tom confessed that he would "cover Marianne with fresh flowers every day" if he could afford it.

"When it comes to love," Tom summed up, "a flower says it all."

It's true. As symbols of romance and affection, nothing gets the point across quite as effectively as beautiful flowers. In cultures throughout the world, this gift is an unmistakable expression of love. In the United States, the tradition has evolved into a multibillion-dollar industry, reaching a peak on Valentine's Day when roses by the thousands are bought and delivered by sweethearts of every description.

When you stop to think about it—or simply look around you in the course of daily life—you may be surprised at how many ways we use flowers. They decorate tables in restaurants, cascade from window boxes, welcome guests to hotel rooms, accompany visitors to hospitals, adorn altars, and are represented in jewelry, tableware, clothing, and stationery. They are part of most celebrations, from Mother's Day to Christmas, from Thanksgiving to Passover, as well as christenings, birthdays, weddings, and funerals.

Flowers say what our voices cannot. If you are like me, you mainly use words—not objects—to express yourself. Yet there are times when words are completely inadequate. When it comes to emotions, I can't always communicate verbally what I feel in my heart. In times of desperate sadness, of unbridled joy, of paralyzing hopelessness, and of excited celebration, the language of flowers speaks to me—and for me. These are circumstances when a single rose, a cheery daffodil, or a bunch of smiling pansies say it best.

I know I'm not alone in this regard, and I've always been curious about the intimate relationship that exists between people and flowers. This has led me to probe this connection deeply when interviewing gardeners. "What is it about flowers," I often ask, "that so clearly speaks to (and from) our hearts and souls? When and why do we give flowers, and what do these gifts say about us?"

"The message of a flower is that while we are alive we should live to the fullest," garden columnist Mia Amato, author of *The Garden Explored,* told me during a conversation in her New York apartment. "Flowers teach us to celebrate our lives because, like them, we bloom and give of our essence for only a short time on the planet Earth before we die."

As ambassadors of emotion, roses and other ornamental flowers remind us of a fundamental garden truth: Life is transient and ever changing.

"I have an amaryllis that will open very soon," said Mia, pointing toward a tropical houseplant with a pregnant-looking bud. "Because of some scheduled business travel, I won't be here when this magnificent flower unfolds itself. I'm sad about that, but at least my housemates will be here to enjoy its beauty. The timing of that blossom is a reminder that, in [songwriter] John Lennon's words, 'Life is what happens while you're busy making other plans.' The garden has its own schedule, its own imperatives, and it won't necessarily wait for you."

A few months before our meeting, Mia had broken up with a boyfriend. The separation was a painful one—the couple had been together for a long time—and the prospect of a lonely Valentine's Day filled Mia with dread. On February 14, she found herself sitting alone in her third-floor loft apartment, staring at a gorgeous sunset and sipping a strong martini. Mia was feeling depressed and sorry for herself when the phone rang. It was Mia's mother, calling to console her daughter whom she had correctly predicted would be having a difficult day.

"As I was commiserating with Mom," Mia recalled, "I happened to look out the window and see a friend get out of his car and start walking toward my front door. He was carrying a single, long-stemmed red rose that he was about to present to me. I immediately got off the phone, of course, and rushed to welcome him. He was simply a friend, not a lover, but he'd been thoughtful enough to remember me with a rose on Valentine's Day. I can assure you I will never forget that kind, simple gesture. It was wonderful."

Flowers do indeed speak a universal language. And while not everyone is as tender as Mia's friend was in expressing his platonic affection or as dramatic as Tom was in declaring his romantic love, there's no mistaking what is meant when we receive a gift of flowers.

Personally, I like to bring along a handful of Gerber daisies when calling on friends, especially those whom I haven't seen in a long time. I've always loved these happy, hardy flowers, and I always feel good when I give them to people I care about. It's another way of saying, "I value our friendship, and I'm really glad we found the time to enjoy each other again." And you never know what will come of flowers that are given away: I have one friend who chose a single daisy from a bouquet, stuck it in the ground, and watered it, only to have it take root and spread throughout her garden.

Another quality about flower giving that I dearly love is its versatility. If you think about it, flowers can be used to express almost anything: congratulations, condolence, beauty, hope, religious devotion, forgiveness, celebration, birth, marriage, death, or for no special reason at all. There seems to be flowers for all occasions. They are one of the most glorious and exuberant miracles of our gardens—a sheer pleasure for all of our senses. And yet they speak just as eloquently in times of sadness, grief, and loss.

I only had smiles and tears of relief when the doctor told me that my friend Steve would not be crippled for life by his accident. I had no words to console the parents of a nineteen-year-old killed in a tragic motorcycle accident. And when I watched my first child being born, I could cry with joy but not speak. Yet the flowers that I carried to others or that were given to me at these times had the power to say with a clear voice what words could not. They were heard by all of us who, in those traumatic, speechless moments, needed to feel love, support, tenderness, and affirmation.

A solemn solitary blossom, a bright bouquet, a perfect rose: they all speak for me when I am tongue-tied with feelings. When happiness and affection overwhelm me, when pain and sorrow constrict my vocal chords, when confusion and disappointment silence me, I have always found—thankfully—that flowers remain eloquent.

Garden writer David Rooks once reflected on this topic when he described flowers as "true messengers of the soul." I love the way he is able to capture their essence with his words:

> God may smile in vegetable gardens, but he laughs in flower beds. City dwellers with window boxes scale their thirst to suffice. But the window box itself holds a chair for the creator to sit, bidding the divine artist: Come, share your joy. And he does. Such simple delights are these, flowers in a box; beauty that would be touched, by scent and hand and hope. Just so, the gardener of souls delights in humble hearts.

There's something affirming and timeless about flowers. They give us hope when we have none. They are playful and mysterious when we feel dull and unimaginative. They restore our faith that beauty will always be a part of nature's plan, despite the relentless inevitability of change and loss. In a sense, flowers say everything.

The late poet and writer May Sarton once shared the observation that "flowers have the whole sequence of life in them, from the bud to the death and then back to growth again. In a way, flowers are all about life."

This sentiment resonated with me when I attended a week-long spiritual retreat in Northern California at Santa Sabina, located in a naturally peaceful setting made even more so by the colorful flower gardens that surround it.

"This place has a sacred side to it and the flowers are indicative of that," Bernice explained. As one of the retreat center's volunteers, Bernice makes sure that the Santa Sabina garden gets all the loving attention it needs. "I believe that flowers are always spiritual and that they enhance the beauty of their surroundings. They are quieting, and they have their own special language."

I asked Bernice about her background and was surprised to discover that she'd come to gardening relatively late in life.

"When I was growing up, my family didn't have a garden," said Bernice, "but my mother often would buy cut flowers. She always stressed that each flower has its own identity and needs its own space. When a friend of mine was sick, my mother told me to bring her one flawless rose. When I saw my friend's face light up when she first saw that flower, I knew that I'd brought her something that expressed my feelings perfectly."

The health-giving energy that radiates from flowers is a gift we all can use on any day of our lives. I'm sure that's why I can't resist buying flowers for myself when I go to the Wednesday morning farmers' market in the city where I live. The world always looks a little brighter when there's a vase of gladiolus on my dining-room table. It's a way of nurturing myself simply by bringing a miraculous expression of nature's abundant beauty into my domain.

I took this theme a step further one morning as I sat in a departure lounge at the Los Angeles airport, interviewing poet and writer Lama Surya Das, author of *Awakening the Buddha Within*. He ventured the opinion that flowers can do much more than help us convey our emotions and soothe our souls. They are also a symbol for the expanded awareness we may feel inside when we spend time in a garden.

"Images of eternal growth come from flowers," this wise spiritual teacher told me. "Flowers are an offering that reassures us that love is much greater than death. After all, we say people 'flowered' as a universal image of full actualization. The word *buddha*, in fact, means simultaneously 'to unfold, to awaken, and to flower.' And in many spiritual traditions, the blossoming flower represents the divine. The significance of a flower goes beyond religion, though. It's much bigger than that. It represents inner growth; it's a symbol of your heart being nurtured and expanded."

My conversation with Lama Surya Das reminded me of something the Sufi mystic Jelaluddin Rumi once wrote. In one of his poems, Rumi pointed out that "there are an infinite number of ways to kneel and kiss the ground." My interpretation of this observation is that there are endless ways to worship and to care for the earth. Or, in the words of another Eastern poet, "to meet the Earth along the entire length and contours of her body." When we relate to flowers as if they are beautiful, fragile emissaries of nature, I believe we open our hearts to a closer communion with the life force that flows through all plants and animals. Through this transcendent process, gardening becomes a much richer and more rewarding activity.

Rucy, a gardening friend and writer, captured this mutually satisfying interaction between plant and human in the following untitled poem, in which she imagines what it might be like to be a flower. I include her efforts because of the sentiment Rucy is expressing; this is a woman who truly loves her flowers:

> I was born from a seed and grew into a voracious
>     plant,
> Part of this garden and intimate in all ways,
> Taking food and water as I rise here in the flower
>     sway.
> Breathing plant energy, shivering down my spine,
> My toes digging in with savory excitement,
> Fingertips growing rhythms as I touch and groom,
> And bury my nose in fluffy blossom.
> That is why the garden sustains me and I, in turn,
>     give it life.
> There cannot be one without the other.

In our gardens, the nurturing and celebrating of nature is often manifested in the way we grow and admire flowering plants. I know many gardeners who put a great deal of energy into growing showy flowers like roses and irises, for instance, simply because they love the way they look—and because they love sharing them with others. Sharing is an essential part of our relationship with flowers. It makes us feel good to bring beauty into someone else's life.

In some cases, the notion of sharing extends not only to friends, lovers, and family members but also to future generations. Some gardeners are acting on faith, channeling their time and expertise into making sure that there will always be flowers in the world for their fellow humans to enjoy.

"My husband and I just planted some lilac bushes last year that we may not live to see grow to maturity," a gardener named Rose told me. "But the idea of planting new life was important to us, whether we live to see them or not. We don't have children, but it's enough to know that someone else's kids will enjoy those wonderful purple blossoms and sweet smells."

Another gardener, a Southern Californian named Diane, told me how she was sitting among her plants and enjoying a cup of coffee one day when a man walked by with his two-year-old daughter, who took great delight in sniffing every flower she came upon.

"So I went out there and asked, 'Would you like me to cut you some flowers?'

"And the man said, 'No, thank you. My little girl is just learning about smells and we've come on a field trip to your garden. Your yard is like Africa to her.'

"'How wonderful!' I said, and I cut them some flowers anyway that they could take along. They stayed for a while and sniffed everything. It felt so good that this love of gardens was being passed along from one generation to the next, right in front of my nose. As they left, the man said, 'Don't worry, we'll never bother you again.'

"'It's no bother,' I said. 'Come up and explore my jungle any time you'd like.'"

It is in this same optimistic and generous spirit that many young people are embracing gardening as well. Millions of baby boomers are now in their middle years and starting to think about the legacy they will leave behind.

A few years ago, I visited my friend Christine and her husband in Taos, New Mexico, where they had relocated in order to pursue their careers as artists. Since both were avid gardeners, I asked Christine how she and Gendron hoped to pass along their love of flowers to the next generation.

"When my husband and I finish building our new house," said Christine, "I've asked Gendron to plant a rose garden. It's important to me because then there would be a continuity from my father to me, and from me to my children, and finally from them to their children. My grandfather was a rose gardener, too, so we'll really be crossing a lot of generations with this plan."

This kind of multigenerational gardening is a wonderful and enduring tradition in a surprising number of families. I know of a woman in Rochester, New York, who is growing a special type of mint that was handed down from her husband's grandmother in North Carolina. The mint plants have been divided and subdivided for nearly a century, with no sign that the process will end during the next hundred years.

Many gardeners tell me that they are always swapping plants among family and friends, often defying conventional (and scientific) wisdom about what will grow where. Such constant experimentation is part of the fun of gardening. In fact, I have a few friends who always seem to rise to the challenge when told that a particular vegetable or flower will not thrive in their climate zone. These gardeners are not easily deterred, having learned through personal experience that they must bide their time in order to succeed. And even when success seems within their grasp, nature can always throw a curveball.

"A garden teaches you both patience and acceptance," my poet friend Rucy sighed when the subject of flowers came up. "You put a seed in the ground one morning in May and wait two or three years for it to get big enough to produce a bloom. Then one July afternoon a bud finally comes out, and you watch this little bloom getting bigger each day, waiting for it to open, and suddenly, overnight, a squirrel eats it."

Rucy has found that, no matter what the season, a garden teaches spontaneity and nonattachment. "You have to be able to respond to what's there," she stressed, "and the fact that nothing is permanent. A garden teaches you that you need to get rid of stuff that isn't right for you. A garden teaches you about birth and death and about what's important in between.

"Blooming is important," she declared. "Coming to fruition is important: to know that if a seed doesn't make it there's always another one; to know that if you reach this way and it doesn't work, you can always reach the other way. Another thing that's important about a garden is its audacity. Seeds will blow in from God knows where, and they'll shoot out of the ground and start to bloom. That's taught me to put my own two feet on the ground and grow up into a flower that blooms—and to be audacious about it."

It's that emphasis on the important stuff between birth and

death—on the vital juice of life—that helps us appreciate flowers even more as we garden. The simple and delicious act of growing or giving flowers can bring us into an entirely new relationship with the world, ourselves, and each other. I learned this lesson myself many years ago when a friend asked me to deliver a bouquet of flowers to one of her male friends who lived in Paris, France.

I was a reluctant emissary. What made the task daunting for me was the fact that I'd never met Axel before and had never in my entire life given flowers to a man. By tradition, I'd always assumed that it was men who gave flowers to women, not the other way around. Exceptions were made in cases of sickness or death, of course, but this occasion fit neither category. The fact is, I wasn't sure what category it fit.

Duty-bound to fulfill Carolyn's wish, while vacationing in Paris I bought a suitable bouquet, then followed my friend's directions until I reached Axel's doorstep. I pushed the buzzer and stood sheepishly at the entrance to his apartment. I held the flowers as if they were a squirming puppy, ready to release them into someone else's arms, ready to free myself of their implied responsibility.

When Axel opened the door, he didn't appear nearly as intimidating as I'd feared. On the contrary, he proved to be an unusually kind and gentle man, with a welcoming smile and a ready laugh. He accepted Carolyn's bouquet from me, the awkward messenger, with relish and delight. The ice was broken.

"What a wonderful surprise," Axel exclaimed. "Please do come in and let us get acquainted."

I immediately felt at ease. Axel and I spent much of that afternoon talking and laughing. We've been friends now for more than twenty-five years. And for over a quarter of a century, we've been exchanging flowers, using blossoms as the currency of our feelings. There never are any note cards attached to these bouquets because we both know what they represent: a deep appreciation of natural beauty and of our enduring friendship.

Many of the gardeners I've interviewed also describe positive memories associated with flowers, sometimes going far back into childhood. Their stories remind me how important gardens are in our lives.

"I'm fifty-one years old and I can describe my grandmother's flower beds in precise detail," a plant-lover named Rebecca bragged. "Every year I go out in my backyard and put in the kinds of flowers that Grandma adored, like old-fashioned snapdragons and cosmos and hollyhocks. As my hollyhocks begin to bloom I remember how my grandmother used to entertain us when we were kids, making little hollyhock dolls out of seed pods and flowers from the plants she grew around her house. When I have memories like that, I can't help but smile."

Even though they may be barely old enough to walk, children seem to register strong impressions of the plants and gardens around them. And as adults, lifelong associations with favorite flowers can build and deepen the language of intimacy in all kinds of relationships. In some cases, these associations can build a bridge to healing and understanding between family members who have been estranged.

"Throughout my childhood," my friend Christine, an

artist from New Mexico, recalled, "my dad grew fantastically huge roses. He had roses that actually looked like those you see on wallpaper. Some of these blooms were eight inches wide! I love my memories of the tall, healthy bushes that flourished in our yard, top-heavy with blossoms."

The corners of Christine's eyes moistened as she told her story. She paused and dabbed at her tears before continuing.

"Now, as an adult, gardening has helped me build a bridge to my aging father. He and I have had a lot of differences over the years, but I've always admired his great skill as a rose gardener. Now we have fully embraced our mutual love for flowers, and sometimes we talk about plants and gardening for hours on end. When we do, we never argue and there are no power plays. The other problems that still exist between us completely disappear for a while."

Although Christine has always loved flowers, she did not come to the actual practice of gardening until her late twenties. It was the magical emergence of a flower from a seed that opened her eyes to the melodramas of creation that could occur in a garden.

"When I was pregnant with my first child," Christine recalled, "I grew some carnations alongside the house, starting them from seeds. It wasn't until after these plants grew up and bloomed that I fully realized that a tiny little seed could produce such a beautiful, fragrant pink flower. It seemed like the most miraculous thing that could possibly happen. So I planted some more, simply to see if the same miracle would happen again. And by God it did!

"Now, in middle age, I sometimes find myself looking at

flowers and asking myself, *How does this happen? How did this marvelous flower ever come to exist?* It wasn't there last month and now this amazing living thing has come out of the nothingness of the earth to bask in all its glory."

I'm sure all of us have shared Christine's feelings of astonishment and wonder at the absolutely stunning magnificence of flowers, particularly those that confront us unexpectedly. This happens sometimes during my daily walk as I pass a vacant lot or a neglected yard. Stumbling upon the perfect petals or the heady perfume of a plucky flower can lift my spirits like nothing else. Such serendipity reminds me that even the most commonplace flower is a living work of art, a point well made in my interview with Melva, whom I met in the charming garden of her home.

"Anything that a person does with flowers is a creative act," said Melva. "I mean, flowers themselves are such splendid creations. Anywhere you find them, even in the broken asphalt of a parking lot, they are so lovely to behold. You can be in just the most unsightly neighborhood and come upon a little tiger lily blooming its heart out. A flower is always something pure and exquisite. I invariably stop to smell them, no matter how odd that may look to bystanders in a busy city. I walk down the street, sniffing my way from one yard to the next."

While we're on the subject of smells, have you ever noticed how the aroma of particular flowers can immediately transport you back in time and space? When I smell roses, for example, I can be instantly connected to childhood memories of my mother. I remember how she bought them only on special occasions and how they filled our house with their sweet, delicate aroma. Those were wonderful times, and throughout my life I've felt happier whenever the scent of a rose is in the air. Many of the gardeners I've met also associate certain plants with specific and powerful memories.

"The smell of gardenias does it for me," said Merrilyn, unable to conceal a wistful smile.

"What do they bring back?" I wanted to know.

"The senior prom in high school," she shot back. "I got a date barely an hour before it was scheduled to start. I had cried so much for fear of being left out that my nose was red and shiny. Yet I managed to put myself together, and I had a fabulous time."

I asked Merrilyn if she thought there was a life lesson embedded in that memory.

"Yes, absolutely," she replied. "I'm reminded that the worst things that happen to you often work out for the best—and sometimes seem like the funniest things later on. They really do. So whenever I smell a gardenia, oh my land, I think about that last-minute date to the senior prom. It was really something."

Barbara Schlein, who gardens in Connecticut, expanded on this idea in a wonderful essay she wrote for the summer 1998 edition of a magazine called *Green Prints: The Weeder's Digest:*

> The smells in my garden evoke specific times of the year. Memorial Day brings the subtle fragrance, duplicated only by #4711 Cologne, of black locust flowers. Occasionally a late May breeze brings me

whiffs of locust flower perfume, and with the smell I am transported back to lazy torpor in a hammock hung in a locust grove, lulled into a drowse by the steady humming buzz of billions of bumblebees seeking nectar 30 feet overhead. Then, while my "past" brain waits for Mother to call out, "Ready for the picnic. Barb?" my "present" brain makes a note to find a new supply of #4711 Cologne. . . .

In contrast, phlox smells fresh and spicy and clean, the epitome of summer flower fragrance. It's a whiff of starched cotton pinafores and welcoming hugs and boundless uncritical affection, of the vegetable garden behind the garage and the pile of dog-chewed bones and summer evening ice cream on the porch in a creaky swing.

One of the true powers of flowering plants, it seems, is to draw us instantly into the swirl of memories and emotions. For some people I've interviewed, the sight of a single flower can immediately bring them back to a love affair with gardening that began very early in life. These are the lucky folks who got hooked early and never let go.

"My parents have pictures of me as a kid standing in front of the tulip bed," Bonnie told me. "I remember being completely enchanted by the many colorful tulips that grew underneath the birch tree we had. There were dozens of them, and those flowers always looked so happy to me. Even at that young age, I really craved a garden. I wanted to fill it with every kind of tulip I could find. In fact, I spent a lot of time thinking about it. I particularly remember wanting to plant the different varieties that would keep my garden full of blooms all through the spring.

"There's something remarkable about that memory. My desire for a flower garden was so simple and joyful. What's wonderful is that you don't have to be rich or poor to make a dream like that come true; you can actually realize it. I just love that."

A different kind of childhood memory—one not so colored by visions of radiant natural beauty—deeply influenced my friend Mez's commitment to gardening.

"I remember looking through a picture book when I was a small child and seeing a photograph of a home in North Dakota," Mez told me. "It was a photo of a white-frame farmhouse that stood in stark relief on a flat piece of land. There was nothing green around this structure: not a tree or a shrub or a flower. In fact, there was no plant of any kind whatsoever. The photograph simply showed the windswept plains and the lonely house. It hurt me so much to see this that I thought, *Doesn't anybody care that it looks so empty?*

"Now you should know that I came from a family whose members talked about planting all the time, who even walked around the yard together and said things like, 'Oh, how about a flowering almond in this corner or a sweet-pea fence over there?' So that's why the image of that desolate house has been stuck in my mind for my entire life. I simply have never been able to accept a scene of such stark desolation completely devoid of plants, and I've behaved accordingly."

One of my favorite personal stories that deals with the

memories evoked by flowers involves my daughter, Nancy, who has always loved plants and now boasts an unusually lush, colorful, and sunny garden outside her Minneapolis home.

Some years ago, Nancy was working as a waitress at a private club that boasted a rather exclusive restaurant. One night, she was called into the kitchen by her boss in order to meet a new chef who had been hired and put to work that same evening.

Nancy was astonished to find herself being introduced to Michael, a man a few years older than her on whom she'd shared a puppy-love crush during her early teens. They hadn't seen each other for years. Nancy's boss knew nothing about this youthful romance, of course, and neither she nor Michael brought it up at the time of their encounter.

After his shift ended that night, Michael invited Nancy out for coffee. Eager to catch up, she immediately accepted. To my daughter's astonishment and delight, she and Michael talked nonstop until the wee hours of the morning. Among other things, she summarized all the important events that had happened to her since high-school graduation. Michael, in turn, filled her in on the vagabond life he'd led as a professional chef, on a marriage that had gone sour, and about his daughter.

The next day, Michael sent Nancy a dozen of the darkest purple-red roses she had ever seen. My daughter was stunned. In an uncharacteristic move, she called me and talked through her mixed feelings about the situation. The message of the flowers was clear: Michael was making an overture, even though Nancy had recently ended a romantic relationship and felt emotionally unavailable. In her heart of hearts, however, she knew that Michael was the man of her dreams. The next week, in fact, Nancy confided to me that she'd often wondered what had happened to this man during the intervening years and had secretly yearned for a renewal of their love affair. It was obvious that Michael had never gotten over Nancy either.

Several months later, after spending nearly all of their free time together, Michael and Nancy set up housekeeping. As I write this, five years later, the purple-red roses—vivid symbols of the most passionate and enduring love imaginable—are still hanging above the dining-room entry of the home Michael and Nancy now share. I am certain that she will never part with that bouquet, no matter how dry and dusty its petals become.

The link between flowers and romance is well known. Much less visible is the role that such connections sometimes play in mature love: the ongoing relationship between two people who've made a long-term commitment. A love of gardening is often shared, although I've found exceptions to this rule. This imbalance can affect the dynamics of a couple's relationship.

At thirty-seven, Gil has been an avid gardener since a very young age. He only recently confessed to his wife that she needed to compete with the passion he felt for his garden, something she'd known intuitively for a long time.

"After I told her how much my plants mean to me, my wife said that she wished that she could be one of my flowers so that she could dazzle me with her blossoms," Gil chuckled.

"Her comment made me realize that there's a lot of similarity in how one cultivates a garden and how one nurtures a marriage or even a friendship. At the core of each of these is an enduring love and affection. Since our talk, I've recommitted myself to nurturing and cultivating my relationship's garden of emotions each and every day."

The point Gil made is critically important. It speaks to one of the most profound truths about gardening: There are parallels between what grows on the outside within the boundaries of our physical gardens, and what goes on the inside within the private spaces of our hearts and minds. I believe that flowers honor what's sacred in a relationship not merely between a pair of new lovers or long-married spouses but also between the various aspects of our inner selves. I'm sure this is why flowers are used by many religions as symbols of spiritual wisdom and self-knowledge. It's no wonder to me that an anonymous philosopher once speculated that "paradise must be filled with flowers."

I am reminded of a story of the Buddha whom, near the end of his life, was asked by one of his devotees to summarize the absolute core principle of enlightenment. "Tell us," the disciple pleaded, "what is the essence of your teaching?" Without saying a word, the founder of Buddhism simply plucked a lotus flower and handed it to the man who had asked the question. The usual interpretation of this gesture is that it showed how enlightenment is available to us in our daily lives, as close as any flower, if we would only open ourselves to the full experience of it. A flower, the Buddha suggested, is a microcosm of all we need to know about life.

For many gardeners, past and present, flowers are powerful symbols of spiritual journeys. The path toward enlightenment, it seems, often winds through the garden.

"One exciting thing for me," a fellow lover of the earth named Zita revealed, "is to stand in the garden and actually watch a flower bud unfold. I know this sounds impossible, but I've done it myself several times. It happens very gradually and you must be exceedingly patient. You say to yourself, *This can't be happening,* but there it is right in front of you. If the day is warm and the light is just right, you can even see the petals slowly moving as the flower opens up. When you come back a day or even an hour later, it's reached a completely different stage."

I asked Zita how she felt after such an extraordinary experience. She pondered the question carefully before giving me this thoughtful answer: "Being witness to the unfolding of a blossom has taught me how ephemeral life is and how no living thing ever stays the same. In many ways, a flower is just like me, changing and evolving every single moment. Yes, it's incredible, but it's also a reflection of the reality of life. If you pay attention to it, the unfolding of our own lives is pretty incredible too."

I've often thought about gardening in much the same way Zita does, and I've even taken her conclusions a step further. If flowers can affect us so profoundly through their powerful influence on our emotions and our spirits, who's to say that we don't have an impact on flowers as well? My own experiences in the garden, coupled with information I've picked up through conversations and articles based on scientific literature, suggest that all living things—including flowers—are affected by their myriad contacts and interactions with other beings. It is this sacred and intricate web of life that our gardens continually reveal to us.

There's a scene in the movie *Phenomenon,* starring John Travolta, that illustrates my point in a dramatic way. Travolta plays George O'Malley, a slow-witted mechanic who becomes a genius after experiencing a bright light. One day, O'Malley is sitting in his beloved vegetable garden, feeling alone and rejected. His neighbors, it seems, are bewildered by changes in O'Malley's behavior. Suddenly, a gust of wind ruffles the leaves of the trees around his house. After things settle down, a look of peace comes over the mechanic's face. It's as if the plants have reached out to comfort him, extending a soothing energy to calm their benefactor. Since their well-being depends on O'Malley's kindness and generosity, his plants feel motivated to help him get through a difficult time. This knowledge pulls O'Malley out of his depression, and he gives the trees a knowing wink and a big smile.

Writer and garden columnist Judith Handelsman explored this intriguing concept in *Growing Myself: A Spiritual Journey Through Gardening.* The book describes how forging close relationships with flowers and other plants may help a person navigate the challenges of life. A garden can "grow" a gardener, she maintains, while the gardener is growing the garden.

In Handelsman's case, the "inner gardening" process helped her cope with career changes, an abortion, a contentious relationship with her mother, and an acrimonious divorce. Handelsman's gardening method is predicated on a respect for plants as living, feeling beings, rather than as inanimate or merely decorative objects. In an infinite number of subtle and intuitive ways, a give and take develops that is based on a carefully tuned sensitivity to shared needs.

"There's an energetic exchange between humans and plants," the author told Susan Gill, in a *Pasadena Star-News* newspaper interview. "Besides cleaning the air, there is an energy exchanged, a healing vibration. The more you tune into it, the more it works."

Handelsman is so convinced that flowers and other plants respond to human emotions that she recommends that gardeners give a plant at least twenty-four-hours' notice before repotting it. This allows the plant to prepare itself for the shock of uprooting. In side-by-side comparisons, Handelsman found that plants that had a chance to anesthetize themselves fared better than those that were given no advance notice.

We can honor the links between all forms of life "like a prayer," wrote Handelsman, by acting upon the implications of those bonds whenever we garden. "Plants are like dogs and cats," she told reporter Gill. "You can communicate with them with your thoughts, your attitude, and your intent. The interconnectedness of all life does not have to be an abstract concept."

There are many spiritual rewards from gardening, Handelsman concludes in her book. The message is that if you cultivate yourself with the same loving care that you direct toward your garden, you will thrive. The author believes that the more nurturing energy and mindful attention we give to our flowers and plants, the more will be returned to us. The same strategy can be effectively applied to many other aspects of our lives as well.

You may not agree with Judith Handelsman's provocative notion that plants respond directly to our thoughts and emotions, yet there's plenty of documentary evidence that our green friends do indeed react to indirect influences brought into their environment. Scientific experiments have been conducted in which seedlings grew at a much faster pace when exposed to Wolfgang Mozart's or Ravi Shankar's music, for example, than to silence or traffic noise. Plants hooked up to sensitive electrodes showed evidence of distress when faced with verbal threats, lit matches, and sharpened knives. One New York City experimenter even found that his laboratory plants displayed a measurable electrical response when he directed specific thoughts toward them from the New Jersey turnpike. Yet even the more prosaic and widely accepted responses of plants to human influence also can yield life lessons for gardeners.

"Someone told me that when I transplant my annuals I should snip off their flowers," my friend John told me. "This plant expert explained that transplanted flowers need to put their energy into developing roots, taking hold of the soil, and getting used to their new surroundings. I considered that advice and then thought about what was going on in my own life. I'd just moved into a new home and felt completely stressed out, with books and boxes piled everywhere. Other friends of mine had been pressuring me to immediately start going out on dates, because I was newly single. But instead, I decided to do exactly what my flowers were doing. It seemed appropriate for me first to settle into my new home before I started showing off."

Flowers and trees are perhaps the plants we most often turn to in adapting life lessons from the garden, but there's no reason we can't discover wisdom in any corner of our yards. Bulbs, for example, are another garden staple that many gardeners seem to learn from. Because they must be planted carefully and nurtured far in advance of their actual flowering, they don't always meet the gardener's expectations.

"My dahlias teach me loads of things," a Washington state gardening friend named Libby confessed. "One year I planted my dahlia bulbs too close to the surface of the ground and they fell all over themselves because they couldn't develop a strong enough root system. The next year I planted them too deeply and it took forever for them to emerge from the soil. The third year I got the depth right, but when the dahlias finally got around to blooming, they were different colors than what I'd had in mind.

"So I had to sit down and ask myself, 'What am I trying to do here?' The answer came back, 'I think I'm trying to impose my standards of perfection on my garden.' From that day forward, I stopped trying to make my garden look perfect. Today, if an orange bulb sends up a flower next to a pink bulb, I'm ready to accept it. There's something absolutely exquisite in this kind of unpredictable outcome."

Libby said that other sections of her garden have taught her similar lessons in subsequent years. One fall, for instance, she planted a coreopsis Sunburst in one of her front flower beds and was surprised when the next spring the little guy didn't turn up.

"I thought it was odd," said Libby, "because this variety of plant is a pretty hardy perennial. A couple of days later, across the driveway and next to a wonderful rock, the coreopsis made its appearance. I have no idea how it got there, but it had chosen absolutely the most perfect place. Now I just laugh whenever I pull into the driveway and see it. The coreopsis looks much better there than it would have in the place where I originally planted it. I'll never know how it jumped over the driveway, but I know that these sorts of miracles are part of an intrinsic wisdom that exists within my garden."

If flowers sometimes appear to have minds of their own, they also seem to be imbued with the divine. For thirty-two years, my friend Toni has gardened on the same three-quarter-acre plot of land. When it comes to filling her flower vases, however, she makes a trip to the neighborhood florist. Like other gardeners I've met, she loves her flowers so much that she hesitates to cut them, even when there is a profusion of them in the garden.

"There are times when I do pick a full-blown, perfect rose," Toni laughed, "but it's rare. When I do, I always take a long look at that beautiful flower and say aloud, 'This is God!'"

Flowers embody the essence of God—or what some prefer to call the "life force"—for millions of people throughout the world. I believe this natural and essential quality of sacredness is one of the main reasons flowers have such wide appeal. They speak directly to our hearts, which I'm convinced is by far the best explanation of why the language of flowers is readily and clearly understood in any country. When we grow, give, or receive flowers, we are connected not only to the shared experience of human emotion—a world that needs no translation and has no borders—but also to the equally universal power of the human spirit.

know I will grow old and die, just as surely as my geraniums.

The seasonal changes that visit my plants teach me about acceptance, patience, faith, and perseverance through the travails and triumphs that are revealed in nature. In the course of a year, I see the entire cycle of life, from birth to death and back again. I'm sure this is why our language is filled with so many season-related metaphors: the springtime of youth, the summer of prosperity, the autumn of our years, the winter of old age.

In our gardens, spring is a time of fresh beginnings. When the tender shoots of the crocus and the first leaves of the tulips poke through the frosty soil, we respond with vigor and anticipation to the assurance that new growth will follow. For me, spring is always an exciting, life-affirming season in the garden, as is the bountiful summer that comes on its heels.

Spring and summer are glorious, yet I know that the decaying and colorful leaves of autumn and the frozen numbness of winter are also times of growth. During the harsh and seemingly dormant months of frozen ground and blanketing snow, hidden roots swell and extend themselves, as plants gather strength for the coming year. Memories of summer gardens nurture our spirits during these cool days and frigid nights. During these quiet, fallow months we are comforted by the knowledge that the cycles of each season— like the rhythms of our lives—hold their own special inspirations and unique teachings. In order to make the best use of such wisdom, however, we must pay close attention to the microcosm of our universe that exists in our gardens.

"Sometimes we are so scattered in our awareness as human

beings that we hardly know what we're doing," my friend Mez, a Minnesota gardener, pointed out during a far-reaching conversation. "Too often we don't seem able to see the way a plant comes up from the ground in the spring—in all its glory and miracle and mystery—the way it grows and blossoms in summer, dies back in the fall, and ends its performance by wintertime. There's a whole philosophy in that."

In order to fully appreciate what Mez was talking about, I sat in my patio chair one May afternoon and surveyed the scene. The geraniums were vivacious and thriving, top-heavy with new blossoms. My succulents and cacti seemed status quo at first. They had been with me for years and seemed almost invisible to my gaze. But after a few minutes, I noticed that one of my smaller plants—a barrel cactus about the size of a softball—was sporting a new spring outfit: a tiny crimson flower no bigger than a thumbnail. The blossom was perfect, yet so small that I had not noticed it until I began paying direct attention to each individual plant.

This experience reinforced my belief that it helps to focus on the constant state of change—the newness—that unfolds in our gardens. I often think of seasons as predictable, bringing with them familiar patterns among plants and corresponding types of weather. Yet I can just as eagerly focus on the fresh opportunities that each season brings. Whether it be a dormant tree in winter or a blossoming flower in summer, the chance to start over again is ever present in my garden—and yours.

Nature is always ready to teach us new lessons and to confront unexpected challenges. Just as there are seasonal cycles of growth and change among our plants, there are seasons in our lives that continually shape our souls and influence our bodies. If we pay attention, these cycles can bring out the beauty of our maturity and the nurturing aspects of our spirits.

My gardening friend Jane has lived most of her life in Vermont, where the red, orange, and yellow of autumn leaves are an important source of tourist income.

"A summer leaf is full of greenness and vitality," Jane pointed out, "but it is only when the chlorophyll begins to drain out of that leaf that it takes on its true color. The chlorophyll actually masks that color so that, in the fall, the leaf comes into its fullness and its real glory. As humans, we need to accept that ripening and maturing are natural things. Our choice is how to respond."

I like Jane's concept of ripening. It can be used as a metaphor for many other aspects of our lives, or our lives as a whole. During a conversation we had a few years ago, TV personality Hugh Downs described maturity as the season of life in which we most fully understand and are comfortable with ourselves.

"I liken it to a piece of fruit," said Downs. "You can go from green to rotten without ever ripening. There are humans to whom this happens, and that's tragic. So it's important to mature and to ripen. I suppose that's what I hope for myself— that I will continue to ripen until it's time for me to go."

After hearing Hugh Downs's vivid description, I was determined that it would never be said of me that I went "from green to rotten without ever ripening." It is one of many life lessons I've learned by paying heed to the seasonal changes in nature. I'm far from alone in this.

"The life cycles of my garden taught me to come into contact with myself," my friend Rucy told me. "I think maybe that's the hardest thing about a garden—yet it also may be the most important."

I asked her to give me an example of this conviction.

"In the fall," said Rucy, "there is a beauty in the aging, dying flowers. This is analogous to what happens to us during the later years of our lives. There's a richness, a maturity, that we have in the autumn of life that we don't have when we're young and green.

"We can be really audacious during spring and summer, when we're green. The flowers are sassy then, too. They seem to be saying, 'I'm going to stand here and be any color I want! I'm doing my own thing here and that's just the way it is!'"

I asked Rucy to talk about the other six months of the year, when a garden may seem to be in decline, or even invisible.

"When my plants turn yellow and brown in the fall, it's like a series of small deaths," she conceded. "But did you know that flowers, shrubs, and trees put down their deepest roots during winter? In the summer, they're gaudy and sensual. In the depths of winter, they put down their roots and gather strength, just as people do."

"Like a true friend," Diane—a fellow Southern Californian—told me, "a garden is there for you year-round. It may take a beating sometimes, but it never gives up—no matter what the season. It always returns, renewed and strong, in the spring."

The Lakota Sioux spiritual leader Chief Black Elk expressed a similar sentiment in a particularly eloquent way: "Even the seasons form a great circle in their changing, and always come back again to where they were."

No matter where we live, the seasons are a familiar, sequential backdrop to our lives. This is the great circle of time that Black Elk and other Native Americans have fashioned their ceremonies and rituals around for many centuries. Although our cities tend to disconnect us from many phenomena of nature, like the nightly spinning of stars and planets overhead, the seasons still speak to us. Yet Mother Nature's voice seems to resonate louder in some parts of the country than in others.

I grew up in Minnesota, a state that proudly proclaims four distinct seasons. Our long winters are known far and wide for their bitter cold, howling winds, and heavy snowfalls. Minnesotans like to brag that their winters "build character," in much the same way that athletes "build stamina" by pushing themselves to the limit during training in order to perform better overall. Some Minnesotans argue that their state's hot, humid, storm-plagued summers build character too. Outsiders, on the other hand, frequently dismiss Minnesota's winters as just plain cruel—and its summers as a frustrating and unending exercise in mosquito evasion. They like to joke that "spring came on a Tuesday and fall on a Friday," bookends to that hellish summer and frigid winter.

Not everybody cares for seasons that are quite as sudden and dramatic—or as fickle—as Minnesota's. Yet even in places where weather changes are much more subtle—like Southern California, where I now live—millions of gardeners are in tune with every movement in temperature, every shift in moisture level. Get two gardeners together and you're guaranteed to hear a discussion of the weather. This is common ground, the foundation on which gardens are built. Without knowledge of the seasonal flux in weather conditions, a gardener can't be assured that his or her plants will behave a certain way. In much of the country, ignoring the average last date of freezing temperatures is an invitation to vegetable-patch disaster.

Our lives aren't much different, since they, too, follow distinct seasonal demarcations of their own: a springtime of birth, childhood, and adolescence; summer of young adulthood and middle-age; autumn of gray-haired transition; and winter of decline and demise.

Author Veronica Ray more intimately explores the parallels between seasons and humans in her book *Zen Gardening*. When we resonate with the plants and animals in our yards, she says, we get in tune with ourselves:

> No matter what the season is, we can learn to be better at participating in the life of our garden. We can find our place in the natural cycles and patterns of the living earth. We can allow nature's energy to run freely through us and use us to be helpful— not harmful—to the garden. We can learn to let go of our human ego's fears and doubts, freeing us to develop our own natural green thumb. And we can carry all of the lessons our garden shares with us into every other area of life, because it is all a single, connected, and continuous energy chain.

For many people, the cycles of gardening are as much a part of nature's seasons as the telltale shifts in weather. As soon as spring rolls around, when the first pale-green buds and leafy shoots appear, you see these itchy-fingered folks coming out of their houses and standing in their frontyards, hands on hips, looking over their plants with the intensity of a hungry bear emerging from its winter lair. If the person happens to spy a fellow gardener across the way, they may gesture to each other and compare notes.

"Well, what are you planting this year?" the first gardener inquires.

"I didn't have very good luck last summer with those columbines," the other replies. "I think I'm going to dig mine up and try them someplace else."

"I reckon that spot is too sunny," says the first gardener. "A columbine needs plenty of shade."

"I'll try the north side, I suppose."

And so it begins: the social interaction that inevitably leads to a friendly exchange of surplus coreopsis or a bouquet of roses or a bag of zucchini. Any of these interactions could be the start of a great friendship.

Like people, plants respond to nurturing, and the month-by-month dependability of the garden can be very reassuring. In the midst of the personal turmoil, stress, and chaos of our lives, it's an enriching and soul-satisfying experience to see a plant do what it's supposed to do, with only the inherent wisdom of nature as its guide.

"This year I had such an extraordinarily good time in my garden," Dwayne—a Minnesotan—told me. "After five months of cold and frozen ground, I went outside, raked the leaves off, and underneath were my returning perennials. I was so excited to find them all! They're like old pals. There's a tenacity and a perseverance among them that I want to incorporate into my own life. It gives me a relaxed and peaceful feeling simply to witness all that beauty coming on the heels of such severe winter hardship."

I asked Dwayne what life lesson this experience taught him.

"Going through this ritual every spring reminds me that there is something about a garden that is so much bigger than oneself. I am left with a great feeling of trust, knowing that nature and its life force will continue long after I'm gone."

Like Dwayne, many people use gardening as a kind of therapeutic lifeline, a calming source of consolation and support. It's an activity that allows them to step away from the frustrations and hard edges of the humanmade world and into the harmonious and soothing domain of nature. The seasons of the garden remind them not merely of the seasons of their own lives but of their human frailty and mortality.

My friend Zelda is one of those fortunate gardeners who seems able to see all of life clearly unveiled in her backyard: from early spring's planting through summer's ripening—and fall's slow fade—of flowers, vegetables, and fruits.

"I can remember being a partner to my grandmother in her garden," Zelda told me. "In the end, a garden is like the planet Earth in miniature. I think about how we grow up and produce children, and how those children produce children. Who knows, with my family's history of longevity, maybe one day I'll be planting seeds in my garden with a great-grandchild. I'd surely like that. It would give me the chance to pass on my appreciation of the miniature Earths we can create in our backyards."

Like many gardeners I've met, Zelda cherishes the time to be alone and to "process" life that is afforded by her garden. No matter what the season, she tries to spend at least a few minutes each day communing with her plants, even if that means simply looking at the now dry and brittle stalks through a window on a cold winter afternoon.

"In summer, I love the nurturing of one's psyche that's possible in the garden," said Zelda. "I relish having that gentle space to pass thoughts through your mind as you're contemplating the curve of a branch or digging in the soil. Very often I'm not really seeing what I'm doing, I'm simply doing it because of that wonderful transference of peace and quiet from Mother Nature to me. That's one of the biggest joys of gardening for me. It's really a time of awakening to the present moment in the busy, distracting world of past and future."

For Zelda, as for many of us, gardening is both a spiritual and a cathartic experience.

"It's a very deep-seated feeling, and perhaps only to be shared with those who are very close to their plants," she said, as we sat on a redwood deck overlooking her terraced backyard. "For instance, I have a whole hillside of ferns, and every spring, during the last week of February, they get a butch haircut. I get all of my frustrations out on those ferns, which happens to coincide with my preparation of my tax returns. When my anxiety level gets pretty high, I go out with my clippers and start cutting. It's the most wonderful, satisfying experience."

Another example of the garden's influence is in its restorative powers. Zelda recalled a ninety-day period during which she lost three close members of her family. Two of these deaths were anticipated, but the third was an unexpected shock.

"The garden did help me a great deal. I would simply go out and work for three or four hours, and it really calmed me down. Sometimes I would talk out loud and think things through when I was puttering among my friendly, soothing plants. Working in the garden has always been a meditative time for me, and during this period of mourning, I inevitably came back feeling more tranquil. Gardening left me neither happy nor sad, but feeling peaceful, calm, and centered."

In every season, there is something going on in the garden that can inspire and engage our senses, our minds, and our spirits. One of the most compelling descriptions of this ongoing relationship was offered to me in an extended interview with Pulitzer Prize–winning poet and lifelong gardener Stanley Kunitz, then in his late eighties. We talked at his apartment in New York City's Greenwich Village, where Kunitz has put together a dozen published poetry collections. His book-lined living space overflows with houseplants, the poet's green thumb in abundant evidence. But most of Kunitz's gardening passion is exercised at his Provincetown home on Cape Cod. I think you'll agree with his observation that the muse is never very far from the spade and the trowel. What follows is an excerpt from our stimulating conversation:

The world of the garden has not been merely a means of survival for me; my garden also has given me something I could trust. It could never betray me, because it responded to my ministrations and it was beautiful. I loved—and still love—the sense of growing things, the marvelous return of one's labors and the beauty of what grows. It's so thrilling to me, in fact, that I can hardly wait to see each morning what's happened during the night.

I used to fantasize a great deal about what would happen to me in my old age. My dream was that I would become a gardener on a large estate. There I would have a little lodge and solitude, and I would work with the earth. Of course, I've been a passionate nonprofessional gardener all my life, so this would have been a very good solution for my problems. And that's probably what would have happened if I had not managed to survive by writing poetry.

I think that if I had been denied [gardening], I would not be speaking to you today. My gardens have nurtured, fortified, and sustained me that much. It is not only a sustenance of the body but also of the spirit within. This is because the garden for me is more than simply a place for toil, it is also a place for meditation and a place for restoration of the inner life.

There is nothing on Earth that I have found more satisfying and more rewarding than those countless hours that I have spent in my gardens, each of which has been, in a sense, sacred. It is in the garden that one experiences the great ritual of existence itself. A garden reflects the whole history of living, dying, and the possibility of rebirth. A garden shows us the potential of a life that is more than mortal, and in that sense, it is emblematic of all religion. There's a kind of perfect beauty in the garden that nothing on Earth can completely satisfy. The dream of that beauty continues to drive one on.

In about 1987, when I was restoring my yard from its previous incarnation as an old sandpit, I wrote this poem about my garden, called "The Round":

Light splashed this morning
on the shell-pink anemones
swaying on their tall stems;
down blue-spiked veronica
light flowed in rivulets
over the humps of the honeybees;
this morning I saw light kiss
the silk of the roses
in their second flowering,
my late bloomers
flushed with their brandy.
A curious gladness shook me.

So I have shut the doors of my house,
so I have trudged downstairs to my cell,
so I am sitting in semi-dark
hunched over my desk

with nothing for a view
to tempt me
but a bloated compost heap,
steamy old stinkpile,
under my window;
and I pick my notebook up
and I start to read aloud
the still-wet words I scribbled
on the blotted page:
"Light splashed . . ."

I can scarcely wait 'til tomorrow
when a new life begins for me,
as it does each day,
as it does each day.

One of the things that gardens teach you is empathy. You develop a respect for the life force that runs through other creatures, other forms of existence, even those that are very humble—and that some might dismiss as loathsome pests.

One lives with mortality every day in the garden. There we are agents of life and resurrection. And when disaster strikes, we live for the promise of the next spring. We immediately begin to think of how to make our gardens even more beautiful the following year. Life takes on a very different coloration in one's garden, and I think that has to do with hope.

In a sense, human beings and the earth's flora are brothers and sisters. We belong to the same kingdom, and we'd better learn how to get along in order to survive together and take care of each other. In my garden, if my plants promise to grow, I promise to take care of them.

There is certainly a degree of sentience, of awareness, among all plants. Certainly, one's plants respond to one's presence, to one's care. One hopes that the flowers nod and say "hello." There is a degree of awareness that the gardener doesn't invent. What I'm talking about is an emanation out of the life process that is receptive to human care and tenderness.

I think of poetry as an art of transcendence and transformation, and I have noticed that I have much the same feeling about gardening. The garden is symbolic of the ongoing life that we lead. It is like memory itself in so many of its aspects.

The garden is a place of private communion. It's very deep; it's very secret. One has a sense of presence beyond one's immediate surroundings. The religion of a garden is between yourself and the universe, with all its eternal mysteries.

For poet Stanley Kunitz, the garden brims with symbols and satisfactions, a true microcosm of life. I, too, witness this unfolding in my tiny balcony garden, perched about twelve feet above ground level along a street crowded with multistory apartment buildings. Yet, like my gardening friends in other parts of the country, I can tell when winter is coming. In Southern California, however, the changes aren't as obvious as they are in the Massachusetts and New York of Kunitz, or the Upper Midwest of my Minnesota relatives.

During the relative damp and balmy winter months on my side of North America, the succulents and cacti outside my living room finish blooming and take some time off. The geranium loses its oldest, palest leaves and becomes rather dormant; the basil plant shifts into neutral. And while it's hardly a picture postcard from the mountains of New Hampshire, some of the trees in my neighborhood turn subtle shades of red and gold and perhaps lose a few dozen leaves.

Even a constricted, warm-climate garden like mine is constantly reinventing itself, accepting the changes nature delivers each year and adapting to the whims of my infrequent intervention. Here in California, sometimes we have a wet winter and sometimes we have drought, or—less often—something in between. The garden does its best to adapt. By watching it respond to the rhythms of the seasons—and whatever attention I choose to give it—my garden fills me with faith in the present and optimism in the future. I know that it will carry on with or without me. The life force of nature—constantly renewing itself—will surely see to that.

There are times when the autumn slowdown of my mini-garden stirs a sadness in me, a bittersweet sense of loss for the heady, robust days of summer, so full of bright, colorful blossoms and fresh, green tendrils that seem to quiver with energy and vitality. Then I realize that perennial plants depend on winter in order to extend their roots and draw sustenance from the soil. Above ground, January's cool temperatures, long nights, and raging storms will test the plants' mettle, winnowing out the weak and bolstering the strong.

Like my plants, I will use the dark and damp months of winter to tap my internal resources and to feed my soul, steadily drawing upon stored energy from places deep inside. During this quiet time my strength will be replenished for the warmer, more active seasons that lie ahead. I know that as I prune my leggy geraniums and transplant my sleepy succulents, these trusty old plant friends are gearing up for repeat performances. Somehow I'm assured that I'll be back too.

The eternal hope exemplified by spring was the focus of an enriching discussion I had with my friend Linda Pastan, who lives in Potomac, Maryland. A published poet as well as a passionate gardener, Linda shared the following verse with me, entitled "Spring":

> Just as we lose hope
> she ambles in.
> A late guest
> dragging her hem
> of wildflowers,
> her torn,
> veil of mist,
> of light rain.
> Blowing
> her dandelion

breath
in our ears;
and we forgive her,
turning from
chilly winter
ways
we throw off
our faithful
sweaters
and open
our arms.

Not long after my visit with Linda, I happened to settle in for a long chat with my old pal Jerry, an avid gardener for as long as I can remember. Over tea and scones in Jerry's luxuriant backyard, our conversation eventually made its way to the garden's marvelous powers of regeneration. We agreed that therein lies a strength that has sustained and even guided us in times of turmoil and need. Then my friend launched into a heartwarming story that reaffirmed my conclusion that in every season, from dormancy through harvest, a garden can teach us important lessons about life.

"One autumn," Jerry recalled, "some dear friends of mine invited me out to their garden for Sukkoth, the Jewish festival that comes after Yom Kippur. I was totally unfamiliar with this ritual, but my friends had a wonderful formal English country garden in Afton, Minnesota, so I thought I'd go.

"The guests were instructed to collect decorations from the garden—fresh berries and sheaves of dried leaves and wild grasses and the pods of flowers and so forth—and festoon the arbor at one end of the garden. We ate our soup outside, sitting on bales of hay, and learned about this ancient religious holiday.

"Our host, Martin, explained that Sukkoth is in some ways a festival of renewal. In a climate like Minnesota's, which can be cruel and unforgiving, it seemed to him that what appears to be the end of something often is the beginning of something else. Martin pointed out that faded leaves were dropping from the trees around us, yet new buds were already setting for the new year. He said it was here that we would find the new leaves and blooms sprouting in springtime. Martin pulled up bulbs to show us how the roots were growing. Then he led us through the garden to demonstrate that, while we thought that life was ending for a while, the plants were really doing their most vital work. Because of things like root growth and bulb setting, Martin assured us, we would see the garden's profusion again the following spring.

"This ritual taught me so much about dealing with loss," Jerry continued. "The experience showed me that in a society like ours, which denies death on many levels, working in a garden brings us in tune with rhythms that are sympathetic to our own human cycles. Gardening lets us express ourselves in ways that our society doesn't allow, including our most intimate feelings about death and dying."

One of the reasons I found Jerry's story so interesting is because Sukkoth is as much a harvest festival as a religious ritual. In agrarian cultures and religious traditions around the world, it is common to find autumn celebrations of thanksgiving for the bounty of nature. They are often paired with spring festivals that mark the time of planting, tilling, and cleaning irrigation ditches, or with summer appeals for the appropriate amounts of rain and sunshine. Because most of us now live in cities or suburbs, our gardens often may be the only places where we can easily re-enact such rituals.

I've found that older people, in particular, derive great satisfaction from the seasonal rites of gardening. These are self-renewing pleasures that change from month to month, following the steady swing of the sun from north to south and the changes in the garden that inevitably follow. As we age, many of us discover that our lifestyles are getting simpler as we let go of clutter and long-held habits. Often we move to smaller living quarters. Yet the rewards of the garden continue, even if it shrinks from a half acre to a single clay pot.

"Losing contact with nature is like throwing gold into the sea and losing it," actor Eddie Albert told me as we admired a patch of mouth-watering sweet corn in the organic vegetable garden of his Southern California home. "Sometimes I walk outside in the middle of the night simply to talk to my flowers and trees—to tell them how much they're appreciated. I might tell the olive tree, for example, how glad I am that it let my children climb into its branches on hot summer days, or the maple how spectacular its colors are in the fall."

In their later years some people, like Albert, use gardening as a source of recreation, exercise, and fresh food. Others develop their gardens as a form of self-expression and long-term sharing, fashioning something that will remain for others to appreciate after they're gone.

"I've noticed that gardeners seem to live a lot longer than most people," my friend John told me. "Most gardeners are relatively healthy and there's not too many of them with any obvious mental problems. You've got to have a lot of optimism and patience. Look at me, I've crowded about three thousand plants onto one little acre. Much of the stuff that you plant might take eight to ten years—even twenty years—before you see the first real blooms on it. You've got to sit back and relax, which is what I've finally started doing.

"I'm a basically tense, nervous person, and when I get out there in my garden, I invariably get calm and refreshed. I think it's constantly healing me and I love every minute of it. I sit there and realize that there are forces much greater than mine at work in a garden."

Many older gardeners have told me that, like John, they consider gardening a meditative activity that brings them into greater harmony with the universe.

"I don't feel the same about my garden as I did when I started," confided Loie, a woman in her seventies at the time of our interview. "Now I really live in the garden and even the house is an appendix to the garden. At my age, I don't 'keep house' anymore, I 'keep garden.'"

Toni, a few years younger than Loie, is clear in her assessment of gardening as a form of meditation.

"I've lived here thirty-two years, and I have found that my garden is now what I enjoy working on the most," Toni told me. "I find that I can totally relax among my plants. I forget that there's such a thing as a telephone or a television. I enjoy the air, the smells, the colors—all five senses are aroused. I pick leaves and taste them. I love the tactile feeling of the prickly cacti and the rough succulents.

"Gardening accomplishes everything that my doctor would want for me, without medicine. My garden provides comfort food for my soul. Poetry that is written on paper doesn't have as much meaning for me as do leaves on a tree or flowers on a stem. Smashing the leaf of an aromatic herb between my fingers and inhaling its fragrance is like a poem."

I love the idea of experiencing nature as a form of poetry. In my own gardening experiences, especially during spring and summer, I've often felt my mind and heart expand as wide as the sky over my head. I believe that the sort of free association that goes on in a garden is a perfect antidote to the stressful world we live in.

According to Lois, a gardener in her late sixties, "The quietness of the garden gives a person space to reflect on what kind of life they have lived. I know that time to be alone, silent, and reflective is not wasted time. My mind quiets and all of my senses come alive. I'm much more aware of my connection with the earth and of nature's intrinsic beauty."

As the seasons shift to fall and winter, the gardener comes face-to-face with mortality. The annual flowers wither, shrivel, and become dry husks. They will not return. And there is no guarantee that every one of the perennials will be back, either, or even the hardiest trees and shrubs. Any of them could die between fall and spring. Yet even during this seemingly bleak time of year, there are miracles.

"In decay and death, a plant still can be beautiful," Diane said during our interview. "When a flower drops its petals you see the inner treasures that you don't see when it's alive. You can enjoy a flower as it withers and dies, and that's true for people too. The seasons keep repeating themselves in every aspect of nature; birth and death are always here if we simply look around ourselves."

Despite Diane's refreshingly matter of fact attitude, I can't help but notice the many ways that our society avoids dealing with death and dying. I am hopeful that a more realistic acceptance of the cycle of life will become evident as the seventy-six-million-member baby boom generation gets older—and does more gardening. I'm pleased to see that the beliefs and values of many of those born between 1946 and 1964 are changing as they grapple with the challenges and choices of midlife, at a time when middle-aged children are dealing with aging parents, and their own mortality starts feeling very real.

I've noticed that more and more of my baby boomer friends are expressing dismay with their fast-lane, rat-race lifestyles and are choosing to follow paths that feel more authentic to them. Many of these friends concede that while climbing the corporate ladder and getting the children off to college have certain satisfactions, these achievements too often leave them feeling unfulfilled and empty inside. Like my close friends Carol and Janet, both in their midfifties, many are asking themselves tough questions: "Who am I, now that I no longer think, look, or act like I did in my twenties and thirties? What's really important to me at this stage of my life? Why do I feel so unsatisfied and disconnected?"

Some of the answers to such queries may be found with the

help of the garden. I have interviewed a number of baby boomers for whom gardening serves as a serene antidote to restlessness, as a source of genuine satisfaction and contentment, and as a refuge from the everyday stresses of work and family. My friend Carol, a fifty-three-year-old marketing executive, speaks for many members of her midlife generation: "Sure, my work is interesting and I'm well paid, but now I find that my daily joy is in my gardening, where I can easily get in touch with a deep sense of sacredness. My garden is a holy place, where I feel truly alive."

Author Gunilla Norris is part of the same age-group. In her book *Journeying in Place: Reflections from a Country Garden,* she described her garden activities as "grubbing-in-the-ground time. Thoroughly dirty from it all, I sprinkle a little earth on myself for good measure. And why not? I am planted in the garden, too."

Some observers dismiss the escalating baby boomer interest in gardening as a mere fad. "Too many of my contemporaries use their gardens as yet another way of competing for status," my colleague Jim told me. "They're obsessed with the latest trends in chic flowers, 'designer' tools, and fashionable overalls."

I disagree. While this characterization may be true of a small minority, my extensive conversations with many midlife gardeners have convinced me that their newfound connections with the natural world will prove deep rooted and long lasting. Gardening touches too deep a place in members of the post–World War II generation to discount their fascination as a passing fancy. The phenomenon brings to mind an insightful observation made by the pioneering Swiss psychologist Carl Jung years before the first baby boomer was born:

> Wholly unprepared, we embark upon the second half of life. We take this step with the false assumption that our truths and ideals will serve us as hitherto. But we cannot live in the afternoon of life according to the program of life's morning: for what in the morning of life was true will by evening have become a lie.

I've been persuaded through my interviews, research, and personal experience that a sizable percentage of forty- and fifty-year-olds are taking Jung's advice to heart, dramatically reshaping their lives in the summer of life, in order to more richly experience evolving goals and values that often are a direct result of midlife transformations.

One doesn't often consider cutting back or changing the shape of a career while one's lifestyle is in full bloom. This applies to our lives just as easily as it does to plants' lives. Yet professional ambition and a consuming career may pull time and energy away from family, spouse, and friends, as well as the inner self. There are life lessons to be learned in knowing when to prune our activities so that we don't lose our perspective or upset our balance.

One of the best assessments of this process I've ever read is an essay entitled "Pruning" and written by my friend Harry (Rick) Moody, executive director of Hunter College's Brookdale Center on Aging. Here is an excerpt from Moody's book *The Five Stages of the Soul,* coauthored with David Carroll:

> Last year, the summer after my fiftieth birthday,
> was the first time we had a decent garden at our
> house. The reason is that my wife finally took over
> the job of gardening. Handing over responsibility
> for the garden was like passing the torch. I noted
> the passing with both regret and relief, as one
> always does in a rite of passage. Handing over care of
> the garden was such a mid-life rite of passage, an
> acknowledgment of my own limits.
>
> Looking back now, I see that year after year the
> garden was always outrageously overcrowded. I was
> never able to weed it, keep up the composting,
> make sure all the vegetables and flowers got the
> nurturing they needed. For years my wife would
> joke that men only plant the seed but then don't
> stick around. I had to admit there was truth in the
> observation, at least as far as I was concerned.
>
> But the heart of the matter was not in abandon-
> ment: I never truly abandoned my garden. I loved it
> and cherished it; in fact, having my garden was one
> of the main reasons we moved out of the city.
> Giving up the garden was hard for me to do. No,
> the heart of the matter was not abandonment but a
> failure at pruning; a reluctance to say no to any of
> my precious plants. Each of those little green shoots
> seemed so eminently deserving of life that I could
> never pluck up anything that had sprouted from a

seed. The result? A disaster. A horticultural night-mare, a mishmash of vegetation fighting for limited light, water, and soil. The garden never worked but it took me a long time to admit it even to myself.

Pruning a garden means admitting there isn't space for everything to grow. Maybe pruning is a special task of the second half of life, but it's one I've avoided for years. Piles of books, half of them never read, shelf after shelf, boxes of files stored in the attic, are testimony to that. . . .

But pruning is necessary in order to live, whether for plants in the garden, or for people in the second half of life. We can't avoid pruning but we can make ourselves sick and die buried in our own accumulated collections, like the mishmash I called my garden for so many years. This truth is as simple as breathing: breathing in and breaking out, building up and breaking down. The cycle of life depends on that rhythm.

In the cycle of life there is a contradictory task for the second half of life: to hold on and to let go. Perhaps old people are destined to be collectors, but how to collect and conserve is another matter. . . .

I visited a friend recently who at the age of fifty had moved back into the house where he'd grown up. His parents had grown frail and been forced to sell the house. When I walked in I saw on the table some carefully tended bonsai plants: tiny trees, just a few inches high. They had the shape of full-size trees and the right proportion of parts. Bonsai exist at their own scale, in a little world that can be mastered and nurtured. Not surprisingly, it turns out that older people are the great collectors of bonsai plants.

There was a message there for me, I realized. Creating a bonsai is perfection in the task of pruning. It requires an act of will to keep the growth of the plant restrained. Instead of picking out weak plants to let the strong ones grow, we take a single plant and accept the fact that it will never grow large, will always remain within its limits. . . .

Voluntary acceptance is not an act done once and then forgotten. It has to be repeated over and over again; every day, in fact. A true artist knows that dancing in a world without gravity is not the way to perfect an art form. And even an amateur gardener eventually discovers that pruning is the secret to making beautiful flowers grow.

Although I'm not a member of Moody's generation, I can fully appreciate what he is saying. In my own life—as well as in the many gardens I've had over the years—there have been times when I've gone through the painful process of pruning. Sometimes this means giving up unproductive activities, saying good-bye to marginal friendships, selling furniture that rarely gets used, or throwing out plants that never manage to flourish. It is a recognition that our relationships to other people and even to inanimate objects have seasons. Our best friend in high school, for example, may have grown into an adult to whom we simply don't relate very well. This waxing and waning sometimes happens with spouses, of course, as well as family members. Even a relationship with a garden is subject to change over time.

In search of other personal reflections on gardening's lessons for midlife, I packed up my tape recorder and set out to conduct a series of in-depth interviews with gardeners in their midlife years. Following are some excerpts from those conversations.

"I'm such a classic type A personality," Melissa confessed, "and I depend on my garden to slow me down. Sometimes my day feels so out of control and its pace is so rapid, but I know my garden always awaits me at the end of the afternoon. Over and over again, my garden teaches me that everything takes time, that sometimes there's nothing wrong with being slow and methodical. I can't find a better prescription at any drugstore."

"Being a super-achiever," Vicki told me, "I used to think that success was measured by the size of my income or the type of car I drove. Now I've redefined personal achievement as having a balance, a harmony, an inner peace in my life. My garden allows me to accomplish this kind of success. It tells me I'm successful, for example, when I turn a tomato seed into a plant that's heavy with ripe fruit, or when my perennials survive a cold winter and return in the spring. And as I've gotten older, my attitudes toward gardening have changed. Gardening has gone from being a chore to being a way of connecting with nature, of grounding myself, and of becoming more aware of what's around me. Gardening has put me in touch with many important things that I lost sight of when I was on the fast track."

"I'm a fifty-one-year-old, empty-nest baby boomer," declared Linda. "I realized not long ago that my life was simply work, work, work. It wasn't satisfying me. I enjoy my job immensely, but it was not balanced by other, equally meaningful activities. These days I consider my garden to be my haven, my meditation, even my health club! It is refreshing and renewing."

"I find that all the cares and woes I bring into my garden drain right out of me once I start puttering around," Robert, forty-three, told me. "I find it tremendously relaxing and stress reducing. I also notice that I become more creative in terms of my thinking, my problem solving. Gardening is very personal and intimate, it's deep and it's real."

"In my younger days, I was a tight and tidy gardener," said Jean, in her late fifties at the time of our interview. "I was bothered by grassy, uneven edges and the most inconspicuous little weed. As I've matured and become less rigid, those things just aren't as important to me as they once were. I simply don't exercise that kind of control in my life, and I am a much looser person in general. I'm sure that my garden reflects the way I've changed during the course of my life."

"I'm a baby boomer and, like me, a lot of my same-age friends are now gardeners," said Arlene. "Many of them say it's a pastime that is therapeutic and even addicting. In many of my friends' homes there are two adults working full time who need some way to relax and feel calm again. Gardening provides that. My own worries seem to float away when I garden. I think about family when I'm out there, but almost never about my job."

"One life lesson I've learned from my garden is that I have to adapt to what my body will handle," said Neil, interviewed on his forty-fifth birthday. "I simply can't do what I did at age thirty-one. That's the reality of aging. Mentally, I think I've learned even more. For example, I've learned that it doesn't take a perfect garden to make me happy; it simply takes my feeling good about my garden, no matter how it looks. I do think about things dying in my garden, but there's always the renewal process each spring. The garden has shown me that I'm not afraid to get old or to grow."

"I think people in midlife are attracted to gardening because it provides a connection to the earth that they've never had," Elizabeth told me. "Everybody seems more con nected to technology these days than they are to the basic elements of sun, water, earth, and so on. There's nothing like the smell and texture of dirt. It helps me feel like I'm a part of my planet, of my universe. It also connects me to the billions of people who have gone before me, tending the earth for thousands of generations. We've made ourselves crazy as a society—always pushing, pushing, pushing—and gardening offers us a life after all that craziness. It's in the fiber of our being to touch the earth, to tend its plants. After all, this is our home—this is where we belong."

One of my final interviews in this series was with writer Ken Druse, who has penned books and articles for the millions who now spend part of their weekends gardening.

"Baby boomers want to have 'the good life,'" Druse pointed

out. "So they're paying more attention to their homes, to their surroundings, and particularly to their gardens. They are looking for peace in a world that is very chaotic—and you can always find peace in the garden."

Of course, you don't have to be over forty to learn the lessons of the garden that come with each season. You simply have to pay attention to what nature is telling you. Gardeners of all ages draw inspiration and comfort from the wondrous ways that their plants respond to seasonal changes—and challenges—in their environment.

"During the depths of winter," Rebecca told me, "I look outside and see the outline of my garden, and I suddenly remember how good the garden makes me feel, no matter what month it is. I gaze out my window at the snow-covered mounds and branches; then I close my eyes tightly and imagine what it all looks like in the middle of summer. Some of my friends try to fill their winter emptiness with shopping and movies, but I don't feel a need for those kinds of distractions. All I have to do is think about my planting in the spring, and I am filled with warmth and happiness."

Lois, another gardening friend, is a keen observer of the subtle changes she witnesses during her daily patrols. "I sit here and am just amazed that so much stuff grows," said Lois. "I'm astonished by what happens during the four seasons of the year, but I particularly love to see what goes on in my garden in June, July, August, and September. Yet each month it changes a little bit, and I'm deeply touched by that."

In the course of my interviews, I've discovered that the seasonal life lessons we learn from our gardens may originate with a single plant—or with some things that are even smaller.

"One year, I sent away for a packet of heirloom tomato seeds," Martha recalled with a smile. "The catalog description was glowing, and I simply couldn't resist. It went on and on about how these were special European tomatoes with delicious flavor and texture.

"So I got the seeds and put them in. The plants came up, and I noticed that they were very late in ripening. But when they finally did ripen, they looked like the tomatoes that you see in the paintings of the Dutch masters from the seventeenth century. They were deeply curved and fluted, and wonderfully colored. In fact, they were the most beautiful fruit I'd ever seen.

"My husband and I would go out in the vegetable patch and turn to each other with the same questioning look, *This [odd-looking thing] is an heirloom tomato?* But in October, right before the first frost, we were able to pick these odd things, and I have to say that they were glorious: the taste, the texture, the contours. My husband agreed that they were just terrific.

"So the lesson for me was that if I waited long enough, if I was patient enough, I would be rewarded with something truly wonderful. It was like a promise of nature fulfilled, and I've never forgotten it."

Here's an excerpt from yet another conversation that affirmed my faith in the regenerative and restorative power of the garden, even in winter.

"A friend told me a true story about an acquaintance of hers, a woman named Sandra, who had become extremely ill," Betty recalled. "It was autumn, and Sandra wasn't expected to make it through the winter to spring. So Sandra had her bed moved next to the window so that she could look out and see her favorite tree.

"'As long as there is a leaf left on that tree,' Sandra said, 'I will hold on too.'

"There was a single leaf that did manage to hold on through the entire winter and Sandra hung on as well. In the springtime, she regained her health completely and was later able to resume a normal life.

"I don't know if anyone, after her recovery, ever told this sick woman that her friend had gone out in the fall and pasted that leaf onto the tree. I guess it doesn't really matter. That little leaf did what it was supposed to do."

Spring's reaffirmation of life is a theme that comes up repeatedly in the course of conversations with gardeners. This is the season that most often serves as a symbolic parallel for our own lives, inspiring us to flourish and bloom anew.

"Spring is a wonderful season," an Iowa gardener named Rachel told me. "The earth wakes up and you do too. When you tend your garden during this time of year, you always get back much more than you put into it. The garden fills your soul with hope."

A garden enthusiast named Ellen said that, for her, spring is a time of strength, anticipation, and almost grandiose delusions about what can be accomplished in the coming year. "My life feels full of promise and my energy is renewed. I love it when the lilies, the lilacs, the magnolias, and the mock oranges arise from their dormancy and come into bloom, because then I know that we've all survived a long, cold winter and that warm, soothing days lie ahead.

"Gardening is the true embodiment of hope," Ellen continued, "hope for things to come that will somehow be better than the past. The seasons of my garden renew my belief that just about anything is possible. I know it sounds crazy, but one of the first things I do when the snow begins to melt is run out and put my hands in the dirt. It really makes me feel good and I suddenly feel much stronger."

My friend Bonnie is someone who, like Ellen, finds something truly magical about the great awakening of her garden each spring. "I pay attention to all those silly—and not so silly—observations that I hear people making about spring and rebirth," she told me. "My garden seems completely dead throughout the winter and suddenly one day you see these little sprouts coming out of the earth. It just gives me a great feeling. Every day I simply have to go out there and look around, and I swear I notice a difference each time I look around. It's a very exciting thing to do."

Iris is a gardener in Los Angeles. "One April morning," she recalled, "I was up at about five o'clock, and the sun hadn't come up yet. It was that wonderful, quiet space of time when the light is very soft and muted. I looked at the garden, and the dew was still on it. It was like crystal. It was so delicately beautiful. Because it was spring, the plants were full of new growth and every shade of green that you could imagine. Experiencing the garden that morning was so very good for my soul, and far too many things today are not very good for one's soul."

Oscar also gets an early start. "I'm always frustrated with facing my garden in the spring," he confessed. "I know it's hard work to turn over the black earth, but I also feel very proud when it is finally done. More than that, I enjoy harvesting throughout the summer. Then there's a time in fall when you help your plants, you cut them off close to the ground and bed them down for winter. I don't feel sad about that—wintertime helps you remember the cycles of nature and it gives you a chance to reflect. It's perfectly natural that the garden goes to bed in the fall; you know it's going to return in the spring. In that sense, I think gardening is an allegory for our lives."

John, a Minnesota gardener, also sees similarities between human beings and their gardens. "Our plants come up and go through all the sequences of spring and summer," he noted in the course of our interview, "then they die away in the fall and winter. The garden teaches us about living and dying, maturing and bearing fruit. It teaches us that if one seed doesn't make it, there's always another one that might."

I carried John's comments around in my head for several days. Our conversation had taken place in midautumn, and as I looked around the city, I noticed people deadheading the flowers and shrubs that had been singed by an early frost. The trees were losing their dying leaves in a steady rain of autumn color. Everywhere I went, the garden was being put to bed for winter.

Barbara, another Minnesota friend whom I interviewed soon after John, treasures the many lessons she has learned by observing the changing seasons of the year—and the way her plants respond to the seasons. On a spectacularly bright fall day we talked about the internal wisdom reflected in the changing leaves and fading flowers of September and October.

"I've learned that plants are tougher than we expect them to be," she said. "You can be a little rough with them and sometimes they actually appreciate it. This has given me a bit of courage about facing whatever lives inside my plants—and in me. Perhaps the most important lesson that my garden has taught me is that if a living thing is given loving attention— whether it is from a human being, an animal, or a plant—the living thing will respond.

"Part of the fall cycle is to cut plants back," Barbara continued, gesturing in the direction of her drooping daisies and chrysanthemums. "Sometimes I don't want to go after the old flowers with my pruning shears because I think it must be hurting them. Yet I know that if I don't cut my plants back, they won't be as healthy in the spring. They aren't as pretty after they get their haircuts, yet if I don't prune and trim, if I don't have the expectation that the flowers will be back the following year, I'll miss a great deal—and I won't learn how to let go of them, or anything else, when it's really time to let go."

Learning how to let go is one of the most important and profound teachings that our gardens can impart to us, along with graceful acceptance of what we cannot change. The bard William Shakespeare brilliantly summed up this life lesson of the garden in three lines which I will not attempt to improve upon:

At Christmas I no more desire a rose
Than wish a snow in May's newfangled mirth;
But like of each thing that in season grows.

# CHAPTER SIX

## Silence, Solitude, and Solace in the Garden

Yes, in the poor man's garden grow
Far more than herbs and flowers—
Kind thoughts, contentment, peace of mind,
And joy for weary hours.

—Mary Howitt, "The Poor Man's Garden"

In our noisy, high-tech world, finding a place to quiet our minds and reconnect with our hearts is difficult—and getting harder all the time. This is one reason gardens are so important. I can think of no refuge from the headaches and tensions of modern life that is more accessible than a garden. In this welcoming and supportive sanctuary, we can begin to rediscover the meaning in our lives. In the garden we can connect to a peaceful and joyful inner core. Here lies our most authentic self.

Swiss writer Minnie Aumonier once described perfectly what I'm talking about: "When the world wearies and society ceases to satisfy, there is always the garden. There is always music amongst the trees in the garden, but our hearts must be very quiet to hear it."

Whether we walk through the cathedral-like forests of public parks or sit in our own backyard, any garden can become a place of serenity, reflection, and rest. When we enter this space, we allow ourselves to disconnect from the distracting and troubling world of machines, deadlines, and petty aggravations. Here is a soothing island of quiet joy and tranquillity. In a garden, we always have permission to be alone with ourselves—and to embrace a world of basic truths.

"Plants communicate universal life qualities to those who tend them," wrote horticulturist Charles A. Lewis in an anthology entitled *The Meaning of Gardening.* "In order to become involved in the microcosm of the garden, one must leave the outer world at the garden gate." Philosopher Thomas Moore, in *The Re-Enchantment of Everyday Life,* adds that "entering a garden is like passing through a mystical gate. Things are not the same on the other side."

My experience has taught me that my garden is a place where I grow on the inside, just as the plants around me are growing on the outside. As one gardener confided, "My garden is where I can explore who I really am, not what my boss or my spouse or my family or anybody else wants me to be." This is why so many of us use nature—as captured in our gardens—

to bring us into a deeper and more penetrating understanding of ourselves.

"It is good to be alone in a garden at dawn or dusk," author James Douglas wrote in *Down Show Lane,* "so that all its shy presences may haunt you and possess you in a reverie of suspended thought."

In both a literal and a figurative way, a garden can help us come to our senses. When we step into our gardens, we are submerged in sights, smells, sounds, and textures. This is a wake-up call for the part of our brain that processes experience directly and intuitively, instead of categorizing and analyzing it in a detached way. When this part of the brain is stimulated, we tend to become more aware of the sensations and emotions that underlie our busy, rational mind. A garden gives us a chance to remain silent and alone with our feelings, to empty the mind of past and present in order to experience more fully the present moment.

"Only in this silence will we be able to hear that gentle breath of peace, that music to which the spheres dance, that universal harmony to which we hope to dance," wrote David Steindl-Rast, a Benedictine monk devoted to a life that balances solitude with social interaction, in *A Listening Heart: The Art of Contemplative Living.* "Let us give to one another that gift of silence, so that we can listen together and listen to one another."

It is in silence and solitude that we are often most likely to discover, sometimes for the first time, what is really going on in the deepest and most important parts of ourselves. We may experience this through various forms of meditation and prayer, or in various activities that still the conscious mind long enough for our unconscious to reveal itself. Through the activity of gardening—or simply being in a garden—we can make the same kind of spiritual connection.

"A garden teaches me about the inner beauty that exists deep within myself," one gardener told me. "I've discovered that one can stand in a garden and it will radiate its energy toward you. It will teach you who you are. It will give you life."

The experience this gardener refers to is difficult—perhaps even impossible—for me to put into words. Because it occurs in the domain of heart and spirit, the encounter with the self that unfolds in the quiet of the garden is better known through direct rather than through secondhand knowledge or verbal description. We must experience "the quiet mind" directly it seems, in order to fully appreciate the benefits of calming the rational parts of our hyperactive brains.

I'm convinced that the profound inner growth that we may encounter in our garden is partly a result of its intrinsic mystery and mysticism, as well as the garden's role throughout human history as a place of sanctuary and refuge.

"Every religion has such gardens," Harry (Rick) Moody, coauthor of *The Five Stages of the Soul,* pointed out to me. "Christianity and Judaism have the Garden of Eden, Islam has gardens underground, rock gardens are an art of Japanese Zen Buddhism, and so on. All point back to a primordial connection: we need the garden and it needs us. It's a gift in both directions."

In many spiritual and religious traditions, enlightenment or higher consciousness are viewed as difficult to attain. By being hard to achieve, these transformative states are made more precious. The walled or secret garden are common allegories: when we finally gain access to a garden's inner courtyards, we see blooms not meant for everybody to see. Yet our secret gardens also might be growing inside of us, if we choose cultivate them. If we open ourselves to the universal symbols in the garden—of mortality, for instance—we can receive (and act on) their messages.

"People today have a great need to return to the soul," Moody said during our interview. "We are so busy, so active, so tied into distraction with our phones, faxes, e-mails, and appointments that we're almost never truly quiet. We're rarely connected to openness. Meditative activities like sewing, quilting, cooking, and gardening are very good at manifesting the soul.

"All that we need from a garden can be found in a single plant, just as in an inspiring work of art. It helps us see what is right in front of our nose not past or future, but today. What we're really after is a condition of simplicity in which the symbols of nature speak to us, and that's what gardens do. The garden presents us with reflections of our soul, with manifestations of God's grand design."

Most garden work is done alone, and gardeners are often bathed in long periods of silence and solitude. There is great solace and satisfaction in these solitary hours, which are a perfect time for reflection and contemplation. Many of us feel restored and refreshed by our gardens, nurtured by the simple miracles that encircle and embrace us. I have found that the sense of renewal my garden gives me tends to permeate and enhance many other dimensions of my daily life.

If I am grappling with a problem that seems to have no solution, or coping with a difficult person or situation, spending a quiet half hour in a garden—even someone else's—can often give me the strength and clarity I need to creatively (and successfully) meet my challenges and arrange my priorities.

My own experiences—and those of many others—have convinced me that the peaceful, nurturing activity of gardening can—and does—help us live much more deeply and fully. For example, a garden can be an important ally when dealing with loss and defeat, guiding us on the journey toward forgiveness, understanding, and healing.

"In times of sorrow," my neighbor Barbara told me, "there's nothing like going out and getting your hands deep down into the dirt. It brings you to your knees, literally. It brings you down to basics. It gives you a kind of spiritual calm that I don't think you can get anywhere else. If you're down or grieving, a garden is a wonderful place."

Diane, a Southern California gardener, especially enjoys the solitude of her garden on weekday afternoons, when time in her yard brings a welcome respite from a hectic work schedule. As a schoolteacher, Diane deals with hundreds of students each day. Her time alone in the garden allows her thoughts to settle and her tensions to dissipate. Picking flowers, watering plants, and pruning branches somehow enable her to act like a carefree girl again instead of a rigid authority figure. In this regard, Diane likes to quote the French scientist Marie Curie, who once wrote: "All my life through, the new sights of nature made me rejoice as if I were a child."

In a separate conversation about the metaphysics of gardening, Libby told me that the solitude and tranquillity of her garden sometimes brings her into a positively blissful state.

"In one section of my garden I have a little bush," she said. "One sunny day I was weeding underneath it and discovered that my cat, Sophie, had crawled into the shade for a nap. I thought, 'That looks so nice, I just absolutely have to lie down myself.' So I kind of closed my eyes and sprawled out, with a splash of sun on my face. A few minutes later I peeked out of the corner of my eye and there was Sophie, stretched out beside me. We both were so relaxed, with the sunshine on our faces and the shade at our feet. I told myself, *Life doesn't get any better than this!*"

Lois, another gardening enthusiast, told me that she starts each morning by bringing a cup of coffee and a newspaper into her garden. "Often I find that I put the newspaper down and simply sit there and enjoy what is around me. I sometimes get teary-eyed because it's such a quiet, nurturing place. I can rest for a few moments before I start my busy, demanding day."

Gardening has qualities that are by definition very freeing, which encourage the childlike and playful aspects of our personalities. We often see "the big picture" in a garden. Presented with virtually infinite possibilities, we may gain clear insight into the path we need to follow. Yet because we are bound by the laws of nature, we must learn to accept that which is far bigger than ourselves.

"I can't imagine life without a garden," Rucy told me. "If you took the ground and the garden totally out of my life, I don't know what would happen to me.

"My strong feeling about this reminds me of my mother. When Mother got really old, I asked her, 'Do you want to move into an apartment?' She said, 'Absolutely not, because then I wouldn't be able to walk out on my own piece of ground.' I understood her feeling, because I think in this era too many of us are really rootless; too many people have left behind their connections to the earth. Through these links, we learn about our planet's essential life force. It's like watching nature's connectedness to the spirit of the world. A garden can't help but give you life. I have a phlox that when it's in bloom, you could probably pick up the energy from its blossoms with an electrical meter."

I asked my friend if she'd ever found solace in her garden during a time of personal trauma or crisis.

"When I was feeling unbalanced or kind of lifeless during the process of my divorce, simply going to sit in the garden was healing," Rucy recalled. "The garden has taught me to come into contact with myself. I think maybe that's the hardest thing to accept about a garden—yet it also may be the most important."

Gardening affords us a deep appreciation for the continuity of nature's seasons and cycles as well as an understanding of the interconnectedness of all living things. Our souls are enriched in the garden by the business of helping create new life, even when things look bleak and hopeless. We come to a greater acceptance of birth, disease, and death because these are constantly being presented to us. There is an appreciation of nature's infinite beauty and intrinsic rhythms as well. We are humbled by our gardens because they teach us that nature has its own plan, which includes us. This design is more diverse and complex than we ever can hope to understand.

The observations of my gardening friends remind me of a particularly eloquent meditation on nature delivered long ago by the English poet William Blake. It is a poem I always try to keep close at hand to remind me of the deep spiritual relationship with nature that can be forged in a garden:

> To see a world in a grain of sand
> And heaven in a wild flower
> Hold infinity in the palm of your hand
> And eternity in an hour.

Not long ago, I met a farmer named Shepherd Bliss who has cultivated a life that William Blake could fully appreciate. Over the last fifteen years, the former Harvard University professor has made a complete transition from academe to barnyard, from malaise to happiness. Shepherd raises chickens, bees, and boysenberries on a two-acre organic farm in Northern California. He lives a simple, quiet existence that draws him away from human contact for days or even weeks at a time.

"I really miss my plants and animals when I leave them to go to the city," Shepherd conceded, on what turned out to be his first full night away from his farm in four years. "I can't go very long without being in close contact with my farm, which is really nothing more than a big garden.

"I love solitude. I honor a deep internal rhythm. I go slow. That's my pace in the garden, which points beyond the self toward a world that manages to sustain us somehow, even though we don't really know how it works."

Shepherd believes that gardens have a very special and even mystical role that can never be reduced to words, that no gardener can ever fully understand.

"Gardens are midway between the ground and the stars," Shepherd told me. "They connect us to nature, and they connect one human generation to another. That's extremely important."

Shepherd encourages everyone he meets to grow at least some of his or her own food, as well as flowers that can be cut and admired in one's house. "It doesn't take much," he assured me. "Wherever you are, plants will grow there, even if it's in one single pot."

This gardener isn't always alone on his Kokopelli Farm. He has hundreds of visitors each year during harvest time, when the public is invited to pick as many berries as they can carry. During other months, he plays host to artists, students, and anyone else who wants to take one of his environmental classes or tours. Through such interactive experiences, he tries to impart some of the passion and appreciation he feels for nature. Over the last several years, many of his visitors have been inspired to become equally enthusiastic gardeners.

"People are often addicted to what I call 'secondary pleasures,' such as drugs, alcohol, shopping, fast cars, movies, and so on," said Shepherd. "One reason is because they're disconnected from the 'primary pleasures,' such as feeling grounded and connected to living things. We are so exiled, disconnected, and spacey in our culture. We need to acknowledge that and seek alternatives. Home is where our heart and hearth are, where we feel warm and inclusive and have a sense of belonging. Most people don't feel they belong anymore. They're disconnected from body, soul, and family. Gardening is a strategy for getting reconnected to the earth. People get rejuvenated by it.

"An appropriate thing for both men and women to do in midlife is to go back to the land; in certain cultures you see this happening," Shepherd continued. "I feel more grounded, more connected to the earth, in my garden. I bought my land from a ninety-three-year-old woman who had been the only other human to live on it before me, except for Pomo Indians. The farm not only feeds my body, it feeds my soul. Gardening is high-touch, not high-tech. It's something that involves the total person. I definitely see gardening as a spiritual practice."

Some individuals—including Shepherd—are natural-born gardeners. They welcome the solitude and solace of their gardens with open arms. I've always been drawn to such people, rejoicing in the positive energy that seems to radiate directly from their hearts. These folks feel truly at home in their gardens and have fashioned lifestyles that keep them in nearly constant contact with the earth. This is where they celebrate life.

"The person who loves a garden," someone wise once wrote, "loves the joys of simple living and the peace on which no one can put a price." Another gardener who fits this description entered my life during a visit to her modest Minnesota farm, located about an hour south of Minneapolis.

We met one afternoon in late summer. Dorothy greeted me with a firm handshake and a bright smile, her sky-blue eyes peering at me from the shady side of a broad-brimmed, straw sunbonnet. I noticed immediately that the skin of her palm had the rough-hewn texture of someone who works a lot outdoors. Her face had the crinkly look of a woman who has known every mood of the sun. I judged Dorothy to be about seventy, though her voice could have belonged to a young girl. It had the high, musical pitch of a songbird, as well as the distinctive flat-vowel accent of a Minnesota native.

"When I'm out in the garden," Dorothy told me, "all I can see and hear are the delightful sights and sounds of nature." She nodded toward the Mississippi River, which runs just beyond her five acres of loamy bottomland. "You know something, it gives me such a wonderful inner peace to know that God has given me all of these things. Surrounded by all this, I am filled with gratitude. I know that some higher power is always here."

Dorothy confessed that during warm-weather months she spends almost all of her days in her expansive vegetable garden, which is bordered on all sides by fruit trees. Each year, she grows bushels of beans, squash, corn, tomatoes, cucumbers, and other row crops. Her orchard yields hundreds of pounds of apples.

"My work starts in March," said Dorothy. "That's when I go through the catalogs, because I like to try out new seeds. After the packets arrive, I put the seeds in small pots, in the basement under grow-lights, and I nourish them every day. I do everything but sing to them. Pretty soon they are growing up and up. When the temperature moderates, around the end of April, I cart the starts onto the patio and watch them grow some more. In May, my brother comes over and tills my big garden plot—the neighbors give me their fine, aged manure. Finally, I put in all my transplants: thousands of them. Then I sit back and watch. I measure their progress every day, spending practically all of my time during the summer working among my vegetables. And you know something, I love every minute of it!"

Working in her garden, Dorothy explained, "is a little like meditating." She bent down to gently crumble a handful of black, fertile soil between her fingers. The dirt had a rich, sweet smell, like a forest after the rain. "You might say that gardening is my way of praying, of getting close to God. I can't explain exactly what I mean, but it's a very enlightening feeling."

Dorothy considers herself "a good Scandinavian Lutheran," yet she told me that her conception of God has been influenced to a large extent by the thousands of hours she has spent over the years in her garden. Lowering her voice as if passing on a sacred truth, Dorothy described a kind of "holy presence" she sometimes feels when busying herself among her plants. It's a presence that infuses Dorothy with a feeling of inner peace.

"When I'm alone out in my garden, all I hear are the sounds of nature: the wind and the river and the animals. The setting of my little farm is superb, with wildlife in abundance. In front of my house sits that beautiful, magnificent Mississippi. Each day, during the growing season when I go back to my vegetable gardens and orchards, I'm surrounded by serenity. I really feel so close to God. Gardening is one of the things I can take with me until my last days, and I think I'm happier here than almost any place on Earth. I feel so good, not an ache or a pain in my body."

Dorothy paused and looked around before continuing. I could feel the inner peace she was talking about. It surrounded her body like an aura of healing energy.

"No artist could paint with the palette of colors that I see in nature every single day," she said at last. "In my garden, I see every color of the rainbow. Being among my plants and trees gives me a contented feeling down deep inside."

In recent years, Dorothy's contentment has been enhanced by an unusual aspect of her gardening. She donates nearly all of her harvest to nonprofit agencies in the Twin Cities area that feed the poor and needy. Every Monday throughout summer and early fall, she fills the back of her pickup truck with ripe, succulent produce and delivers this bounty to food banks and homeless shelters.

"It's so rewarding," said Dorothy, noting that most of the donated food is consumed by children, single mothers, and the low-income elderly. "Everyone needs to eat, and I happen to know how to grow things. Through my work in the garden, my life feels worthwhile."

Of course, most of us can't live like Dorothy. Our gardens have to be squeezed into yards in the cities, small towns, or suburbs where most of us live. The wonderful thing about gardening is that its greatest rewards are accessible, one way or another, to each and every one of us—including children.

My friend Lynn once told me a remarkable story about her

son, Mike, who was seven years old at the time. On this particular day, the second grader came home from school feeling that he had alternately been scoffed at and ignored. A series of events had left Mike feeling frustrated, inadequate, and angry. Sensing that her son was in need of some tender, loving care, Lynn convinced Mike to accompany her on an impromptu outing to a "secret garden," a lush compound maintained by a spiritual group not far from their Pacific Palisades home.

"I didn't say anything at first," Lynn recalled. "We just walked among the flowers. We sat down next to a small lake and watched the breeze blowing through the boughs of the tall trees that encircled it. Finally, Mike turned to me and whispered, 'This place is so beautiful!'

"When I asked why he was whispering, Mike told me that he thought he shouldn't say such a thing at all, 'because real men don't do that.'

"I looked him straight in the eye and said, 'Smart men do.' Then he started opening up and talking about what his problems were. It turned out to be a very special couple of hours that we've never forgotten, even though Mike is a grown man now with a child of his own."

I asked Lynn why she thought the experience had helped her son open up to her.

"Mike had never been to a place like that," she speculated, "and it touched him in a very special way. I'd never been at his side in such a serene place, and that touched his soul. Now, as an adult, Mike and his wife are passionate gardeners who are enormously happy whenever they get a chance to sit and enjoy nature."

I wondered how the afternoon with her son has affected Lynn's own relationship with gardens and gardening. She sat thoughtfully for a few moments before answering.

"I now have only a small patio garden, about twelve feet by fourteen feet in size," she replied. "Yet I continue to seek out solitude there. My garden has always been a place of refuge and retreat, the place I go to sit and think whatever thoughts come into my mind. I don't answer my phone or sort through my mail; I just go there and sit and unwind. Sometimes I don't even change my clothes after I get home from work, I simply go out on the patio and putter around. The garden is my escape, my comfort.

"As I've grown older," Lynn continued, "trees have become more important to me; the sheltering boughs surround me like the arms of God. I often stop to hug or stroke a tree and this makes me so happy. I feel very spiritual when I'm out in the forest and hiking around. I'd like my ashes to be scattered among the trees in the mountains, because the connection with the universe is there. In my garden, the roots go into the earth and connect with other roots, as people connect with other people. That's a reminder that all living things are really part of one whole."

Nancy Forrester is a much different sort of gardener, cultivating a large plot of land at the southernmost tip of Florida, yet she finds the same sort of solace and solitude among her jungle plants as Lynn does on her patio. Nancy's Secret Garden is a semiprivate sanctuary in Key West that has become an inspiration to hundreds of visitors.

"I don't meditate or pray," Nancy told me, "but I've felt a

tremendous need to stay connected to what I call 'the sense of the wild.' For me—and maybe for all human beings—it's a cellular or genetic thing. My garden was never just about growing plants, it has always been about learning about life from the mysteries of nature."

Several decades ago, before Key West, Florida, became the major tourist attraction it is today, Nancy bought an acre of land that is now the biggest undeveloped parcel (and last vestige of greenery) in the downtown area. She planted dozens of varieties of palm trees, along with hundreds of tropical flowers, vines, bromeliads, and shrubs. More than 150 species of plants are found here, including some that are considered rare and exotic. In the middle of this verdant tropical paradise is her modest home, gallery, and studio, where she paints and teaches art. Nancy maintains the garden as an inspirational nature sanctuary for plants and animals, including humans.

"Art and spirit and plants are pulled together in gardening for me," said Nancy. "These things visually, aesthetically, and sensually nourish me in this environment. It's a garden that's not meant to be experienced cerebrally, but to be felt in the heart, soul, and spirit. Nothing in the garden is labeled because I want people to stay connected to this green space through feeling, not thinking. You walk on the paths and you linger. When you take that journey, I hope that you'll meet yourself. I hope that your heart will open."

Nancy told me that she has absorbed a great deal of "universal knowledge" from her miniature rain forest. I asked her to explain.

"I get a lot of my energy from the garden," she told me. "I

seem to lose that force—that energy—when I go downtown and my senses are not in touch with nature any more. I am revitalized by my garden in a powerful way. As a young person, I was always drawn to the interrelatedness of all life-forms, and I often painted pictures that dealt with this. I suppose I'm kind of a mystic, because I love the mystery of life, the spirit that inhabits all living things."

Nancy feels deeply connected to the solace and solitude she experiences in her Key West garden. Her situation is somewhat unusual in that her lifestyle has allowed her to live alone (not counting a collection of gregarious parrots) on a wild, previously undeveloped tract of land for over thirty years, successfully integrating this environment with her career as an artist. Yet I have met dozens of gardeners who feel a similar kind of connection with their plants, even though they commute to offices, raise children, and follow a more traditional pattern of living in a modest house or a city apartment.

My conversation with Nancy Forrester reminded me of my meeting with Sheila, a college professor and the wife of one of my colleagues. I caught up with Sheila just as she and Bob were about to relocate from Ohio to Colorado. Sheila conceded that she would miss the garden she had cultivated for the previous ten years, but emphasized that her greatest satisfactions as a gardener come from quiet contemplation of Mother Nature, wherever she might appear.

"I often will just sit down on the ground and watch insects, like bees, moving around," said Sheila. "I find them to be interesting and friendly characters, even when they buzz right in my face. It's fun to watch them in a spirit of wonderment.

Another endless source of pleasure is watching a flower emerge. One day it's a bud, the next it's a flower. I also wonder why some plants thrive and some don't."

Sheila grew up on a farm in Kansas and has always felt attached to growing things. Before she married and moved out of her apartment, she had built up a collection of over one hundred houseplants. She now spends several hours every weekend tending the greenery that surrounds her home. I asked Sheila what grows inside of her as she watches the garden grow outside of her.

"Patience, relaxation, a feeling of oneness with the universe," she replied. "I feel a total sense of transcendence, a connection with nature and with future generations that is completely nonpersonal. Gardening puts me in touch with the universe, and with my being, my soul, that part of me that is beyond my mind and my body. I have a deep sense of peace in my garden: not every single moment, but regularly. There is often a slowing down inside and a feeling like, *This is God's work. I'm his tool, his instrument.*"

Sheila shared a poem that her husband had written for her one morning after watching her work in the garden. Bob captured Sheila in the golden glow of dawn, completely absorbed in a loving communion with nature. His poem—which was penned solely as a gift to Sheila—is called "Ballet of the Garden":

> Bright early-morning sun glints from golden hair
>     as she bends deeply to reach the lowest flowers.
> Her angular face is serene and beautiful, a reflection
>     of relaxed yet supreme concentration.

> Her delicately muscular arms reach lovingly as she
> moves quickly and easily from stem to stem.
>
> Her strong hands prune and discard dead blossoms
> with the practiced graceful motion that is her
> unique, unconscious dance.
>
> It is her body's way of celebrating with subtle beauty
> the profound well-being that comes from the
> moment-by-moment wholeness of body-mind-
> spirit-earth-sun-sky.

"I'm so in awe that he did this," said Sheila, when I asked for her reaction to Bob's poem. "It says that he noticed what I love about the garden."

The notion that tending the earth also mends the spirit comes as no surprise to the many gardeners who equate the silence and solitude of their gardens with caring for one's mind, body, and soul. Another writer and poet who finds spiritual fulfillment and quiet solace in gardening is Betty Sue Eaton, author of *Listening to the Garden Grow: Finding Miracles in Daily Life.* She spent much of her adult life raising a family in Nevada before moving to Utah with her husband after their children were grown. A devout Christian, Betty Sue has found her faith strengthened and expanded through her relationship with gardening, which is what she writes about in her book. As with many gardeners I've talked to, Betty Sue feels close to the creative forces of the universe when she spends time among her plants.

"I hear God at work in my garden," Betty Sue told me. "I feel that a seed is one of life's greatest miracles. In the Bible, faith is equated to the grain of a mustard seed. It just grows and grows. That's how I feel about what I plant. I share it, use it, save it; it just goes so much further than simply putting that little seed in the ground."

Betty Sue began gardening "out of necessity." She and her husband, Grover, were newly married and Betty Sue was having difficulty finding work in her field: teaching business at the college level.

"I felt guilt ridden because I wanted to do something to help," Betty recalled, noting that she and her six siblings always had been told to do their fair share. "My husband agreed to help me put in a garden, so we proceeded to pull out some of the back lawn and put in a watering system. I felt the rewards of gardening soon after I began: the peace and quiet that comes from actually communing with the Lord every day."

Betty Sue's involvement with gardening soon went beyond the boundaries of her backyard.

"Whenever I had a plant that did well, I'd find someone to share it with," she explained. One of the first neighbors Betty Sue shared her bounty with was an eighty-two-year-old neighbor named Helen, who was suffering from a terminal disease and greatly appreciated the gift of fresh flowers and vegetables every day.

"She'd peer over my fence and say, 'I think I'm looking at paradise; this must be what heaven looks like.' A couple of days before her death, Helen and her husband came over and walked through the garden so that Helen could see it up close one last time. She thought the garden was a world unto itself, a jewel. This lifted my spirits so much."

The Eaton's only son was diagnosed with renal cancer at age forty-two. At the time, Richard was having great difficulty with his teenage son, Barrett, who had dropped out of school amid great personal turmoil. In a spiritual rebirth, Richard became a devout and active churchgoer. Sadly, his troubled son died in a car accident, and shortly thereafter, Richard himself was claimed by cancer. During this stressful time, Betty Sue spent many mornings in quiet meditation on the patio of her Las Vegas home.

"Sometimes I'd marvel about what the garden can do," she told me. "Other times there'd be a quiet sadness. The garden provided solace. It was now much more than a hobby; it became an actual connection between me and nature and God. The garden became something like a chapel."

Betty Sue cannot imagine what she would have done during that terrible period without her quiet garden to help her rebuild "and realize that there are seasons that need to be fulfilled." She told me that getting older has significantly affected her relationship to her garden—and to life itself.

"I don't want to put things off anymore," she stressed. "I want to do what's important now. My plants will be around only for a short time and my own time is brief too. I don't mind that. It gives me a deeper appreciation of beauty and my need to get the most out of everything, including my garden.

"A garden is God's metaphor for life. It has its seasons, just as we do. If we look and imitate what the garden does, our seasons will pass with as fine a rhythm as the garden's. We do beautifully if we follow the wisdom that we see in the garden and don't reject what comes along naturally. It's a challenge, but we can be as beautiful in spirit as our gardens are."

Betty Sue Eaton's use of her garden as a means of reaffirming her Christian faith is an example of one of the many ways in which nature can help us navigate life's difficult passages. Although not everyone chooses to use the term *God* when referring to a divine entity or presence, many of us, like Betty Sue, find that our relationship with the sacred is deepened and strengthened by contemplative time spent in the garden. For some people this kind of spiritual connection exists within a formal religious tradition, while for others, it is entirely secular. In the course of my conversations with gardeners, I've found that the distinction is irrelevant. What matters is how people choose to make use of this spiritual connection in their daily lives.

My friend Tom encounters the power of the spirit not through a church but through growing things. "In my faith," he explained, "heaven and earth are connected. I believe that God's grace and bounty come through the earth, which may be why I've maintained a garden in every place I've ever lived. This is my way to touch the creative force of nature, to get away from the hubbub and noise of modern civilization."

Since childhood, Tom has sought refuge in what he calls "secret gardens." At age six, his family moved to the country and took up residence on twelve hundred acres of farmland.

"I explored the area and found places where I was certain that pixies and gnomes lived: nooks and crannies among the creeks and trees where no one had ever gone. I'd sit and wait for the elves to show up. I never saw any, but I knew they were around. These places were my special sanctuaries where nobody could encroach, especially adults. When things were bad at home, they were the only places I could go for peace and comfort. This is where I became revitalized and ready to take on the next battle. I was the only one who knew where these places were. As a matter of fact, I still am."

Tom turned to nature many years later, as an adult, when his parents died. Although he had long since moved away from the farm, Tom returned to his secret gardens to sort out his feelings about the loss of his mother and father. "It gave me great comfort to know that the natural world would still go on, even though my parents were gone. I was able to say good-bye to them."

The experience brought back one of Tom's favorite memories from childhood. On his way to elementary school, he would walk past a house that had a bed of pansies. He'd pick them to bring a few home to his mom, as a symbol of his love and gratitude. Tom laughs at the memory now: "My mother was always gracious in accepting them, even though she knew I had stolen them."

My friend faces a different set of challenges today. In the prime of midlife, Tom contracted a debilitating disease that confines him much of the time to a wheelchair. Yet even this disability hasn't discouraged him from gardening.

"My wife has made raised beds for me to cultivate. She knows that I've always grown flowers and always will. I think they're the most beautiful things in the world. Flowers and gardens to me are symbols of what's precious and important in life. It's very much the way we're made: with one bright, beautiful, shining moment. We have to make the best out of every second we have on Earth. It bothers me that people don't realize the full significance of that."

The magical outdoor sanctuaries of Tom's childhood changed his life. Similar kinds of changes are going on in secret gardens all over the United States and the rest of the world.

I know of one gardener—who is adamant that neither she nor her garden be identified—who has created a very special garden that honors children, and the child that lives inside all of us. Her garden is full of delightful and often whimsical statuary, altars, hand-lettered signs, and found objects. Embedded in the cement of the garden's walkways, walls, and benches are small, glittering crystals, toys, mirrors, amulets, and icons. The garden is abloom with flowers and lush with semitropical foliage. Many visitors have left whimsical (and very personal) mementos among the trees and flowers, along with inspiring words inscribed on plaques and in the pages of a guest book. Here are some excerpts:

> "What a magical place! I thought gardens like this only existed in dreams. Thank you for this beautiful gift."

> "In a garden there are no strangers. There's no them, only us. The world is one garden, the garden of us."

> "Thanks. I needed this. Wish I could stay longer."

> "My best friend brings me here to celebrate.

Celebrate what? Anything! And to give apprecia-
tions."

"He who works in a garden works hand-in-hand
with God. How evident that is here."

One of my favorite signs in this "secret garden" shared this
quote attributed to Claude Monet, whose impressionist
paintings of his French garden are timeless masterpieces: "I
paint so I can have money to buy plants."

The almost mystical quality of this secret garden makes it a
wonderful place to meditate, to sit quietly and absorb the
positive, life-affirming energy that it emanates. I feel very fortunate to have been allowed to see this unique place, which is
never publicized and is accessible by invitation only. The
owner declines all interview requests. Her garden is fitting
tribute to the spiritual nature of humans, and it means a great
deal to me that someone would selflessly dedicate so much of
her life to its creation.

Some of the gardeners I've spoken with prefer to use the
term *personal* rather than *secret* to describe their private outdoor sanctuaries.

Curt is a biologist in his midfifties who confessed to me that
less than five years prior to our interview he "couldn't have
cared less" about gardens and gardening. Now he has created
two very personal gardens in separate parts of the yard that
surrounds his Southern California home. One garden is
Oriental, the other is African, blending and reflecting the
main design elements of the house.

"I love to sit in my gardens, and I spend a great deal of time in them," said Curt. "The Oriental is between the kitchen and the den, and it has sliding glass doors so I can go through it whenever I want. It has a bench where I can sit and contemplate. I find a lot of serenity in my Oriental garden. It's my getaway. It only has green foliage, no distinct flowering plants except an orchid.

"My patio garden is much the same," Curt continued, "only I have a view of a lake from there. So I have nature with me whenever I'm home. As I've gotten older, I've found that I enjoy spending more time at home, which is how gardening has become such a passion for me. It's also brought a spiritual deepening into my life. I can spend a lot of time just looking at things in nature and how they're arranged. It's meditative, I suppose, although I've never thought of gardening as a form of meditation. But it's at least deep observation. I'll look at the creases in the rocks for what seems like hours, and then move on to examine every single new leaf and shoot on my plants. The adoption of plants into my life—I previously ignored them—has been a very big shift for me. The change just happened; I didn't plan it."

The premise of this book is that life is full of lessons and a garden is one place to learn them. Yet one must be receptive to these lessons in order to hear them, which may explain why Curt developed his interest in gardening so suddenly. Until he was ready and willing to listen, he could not hear what a garden has to say. His transformation reminded me of the ancient Chinese aphorism: "When the student is ready, the teacher will appear."

Throughout my own life I have found that the silence of my gardens helps me quiet the thoughts of my rational mind. I feel immense relief in abandoning, at least for a short time, my brain's attempts to overly control or plan my future and to analyze or mull over my past. As I prune and transplant—or quietly sit and admire my plants and flowers—I transfer my focus to what's right in front of me, here and now. This shift in attention may sound simple, yet its implications are profound and far reaching. Spending a half hour in nature, I've discovered, often can restore my energy when I'm tired, lift my gloom when I'm depressed, and open my heart when I feel abandoned.

There is no other teacher quite like nature. What it teaches us is different than what we learn in schools, churches, museums, concert halls, or sitting around our dinner tables. As manifested in the garden, nature puts us directly in touch with a world that operates not according to humanmade laws, but according to the laws of creation. When we make direct contact with that world, we are instructed at all levels of our being. It may come as a surprise that we don't have to go any farther than our yards to make that connection.

Leon Whitson, author of *The Garden Story,* lives and writes in a modest home in West Hollywood, California. His book is a long, eloquent essay about the transformation of his neglected, desolate quarter acre into a peaceful, beautiful refuge. More important, *The Garden Story* describes the journey of self-discovery that Leon undertook in the process of creating this soothing green sanctuary.

"My heart is hammering for reasons I can't define," Leon

wrote, shortly after the garden overhaul was complete. "There are goose bumps on my skin as I tune my ear to the garden's intimate resonances. I know this place so well, yet it always startles me with its fresh nuances of shade and light, its fugue of smell sharp and sweet, its range of textures rough and smooth, its melody of sounds delicate and dangerous."

A fiction writer and an architecture critic as well as an essayist, Leon began gardening in earnest when he became bogged down in the course of writing a new novel.

"Once I had learned to listen to my garden, to hear the rhythms of its life as well as to take in the symphony of its sounds, smells, and sights, I was rewarded with a fresh wave of inspiration," Leon wrote.

In short order, his novel was completed. "New life blossomed in the ruins of my confidence as a writer. My nurturing fostered the garden's regeneration, and in turn, the garden's new growth recharged my courage. I helped it live and it helped me live. And I began to write yet another novel. The creative energy flowed both ways."

Eager to learn more about the source of this verve and inspiration, I called Leon and introduced myself. He graciously agreed to take me on a personal tour of his garden. I arrived a few days later and found myself charmed by his infectious enthusiasm and unusual accent. (I later learned that Leon was born and raised in the African nation of Zimbabwe, the former British colony of Rhodesia.)

"There are actually five separate 'rooms' in my garden," he told me, as we stepped into a particularly sunny area of Leon's backyard that was enclosed by a diamond-shaped perimeter of shrubs and hedges. "Dividing a small yard into several distinct 'rooms' is an architectural trick designed to make the overall space seem larger than it really is."

Leon led me from one room to another. I immediately noticed the distinctive ambiance that pervaded each. One area, for instance, was dominated by sacred symbols from various religions: a Native American sun, a Tibetan Buddha, the entwined snakes of ancient Greece, Rome's goddess of wisdom, Minerva, and god of wine, Bacchus. Another section of the garden was cool and dark, deeply shaded by broad-leaved tropical plants, a lemon tree, and an enormous bougainvillea vine. In this quiet corner was a fountain, next to which Leon would often sit and meditate or listen to classical music.

As we moved from one enclosed space to another, my host pointed out individual plants that he had acquired from friends over the years, each a reminder of a certain personality.

"The most emotionally stirring are the plants that I've gotten from people who died, including three of my friends who had AIDS. Just before each of them died, they realized they weren't going to be able to take care of the plants, and they gave them to me. So each one reminds me of that dimension of that particular friend. Somehow that part of them goes on living as I tend to their plants. For example, I have a pomegranate tree that was given to me by a man who died of AIDS in his thirties. When he gave it to me, the tree itself was dying. I replanted it and worked very hard to revive it. Now it's flourishing and giving of its blood-red fruit, which is very poetic. So a vital aspect of my departed friend is still a constant in my life."

Leon said that sometimes, if he's feeling a bit low, he retreats to his garden and sees how his plants are thriving. "I seem to pick up some of the unstoppable life force that they seem to have. I feel nurtured by them. I tend my garden as a parent takes care of a child, and I get unconditional love in return. Another aspect of gardening is that it strikes me as a very childlike activity. You use very simple implements, and you can play in the mud without looking foolish."

My tour convinced me that Leon had indeed turned his garden from a desolate to a magical place. Something very neglected now looks extraordinary.

"For someone who had never gardened before buying this house," he said, "this accomplishment has been very encouraging to me. It's made me much more human. Creating my garden has also helped me understand something about the nature of creativity itself: you have to stop trying to control it overtly and allow it to develop on its own terms. When you create something that has its own validity, its own life, you have to listen to that life and the direction it wants to grow in. In other words, you can't force things to happen when or how you want them to happen, they have a natural rhythm of their own."

Leon said that one of the important life lessons his garden has taught him is the art of listening. In a culture based largely on assertiveness and selling, listening is in short supply. His garden, according to Leon, had helped him learn to listen not only to actual physical sounds—like birds trilling and fountains splashing—but also to internal voices.

"You carry your own Eden inside you," said Leon, "the

place outside of you that somehow links to what's inside. You can encounter that Eden almost anywhere. I've found landscapes in Spain and Greece that are like that for me, although my present yard in West Hollywood is definitely the most powerful link I've ever known.

"I have become so passionate about such benefits," Leon concluded, "that my garden has become vital to my survival at this point. I think that's because its tending requires getting at what is below the surface, to all sorts of hidden meanings and metaphors. Our daily lives are filled with a lot of trivia and unimportant things, but a garden is always completely real."

Visiting Leon's garden and hearing him speak so articulately about its metaphysical rewards was a balm to my soul. *Here is a man,* I thought, *who has been wonderfully transformed by his garden.* The experience reminded me that the relationship between gardener and garden is intensely personal. No two gardens are alike, just as no two people are ever the same. In a very real sense, when you make a garden, you create your own reflection in the natural world. It is through the process of thoughtfully studying this image, shaped and shaded by nature, that we have the chance to learn a great deal about our inner selves.

I sometimes wear a T-shirt inscribed with the following statement: "Everything I need to know about life I learned from gardening." The message may be lighthearted, but it is also very real. I am persuaded that the spiritual guidance and powerful insights that grow within us as we tend our gardens do, indeed, have the power to change our lives for the better.

I'm convinced that a well-tended life can flourish and prosper just as a garden thrives and expands when lovingly cared for. The virtues of balance and patience, silence and solitude, diversity and respect, are all manifested in our gardens—if we simply pay attention to the natural rhythms that keep them alive and well. Perhaps the greatest virtue offered by a garden is the importance of minimizing distraction in our lives, of slowing us down enough to truly feel and listen. By taking time in a garden to embrace silence and solitude, we are able to fully appreciate the present moment. It is in this moment that we are authentically living life.

"My garden flourishes in silence and shrinks amidst distraction," Vivian Elisabeth Glyck pointed out in her lovely little book, *Twelve Lessons on Life I Learned from My Garden: Spiritual Guidance from the Vegetable Patch.* "By watching things grow, I can turn down the noise in my brain and observe firsthand the miracle of mindfulness. The absolute cycle of birth, death, and renewal displays itself before me, and I find that I can be completely present in a way that I never before have been. . . . I can allow things just to be, and with only a helping hand from me, a large force manages the whole game."

Since we, as humans, are an integral part of nature, we can never successfully separate ourselves from it. Yet our preoccupation with technology and machines relentlessly pushes us away from the natural world. When nature speaks to us—through the silence and solitude of our gardens and parks—we are told the fundamental truths of our planet, of our very existence. This is why it is so important to quiet our minds and listen.

CHAPTER SEVEN

# Where Do We Grow from Here?

People usually consider walking on water or in thin air
a miracle. But I think the real miracle is . . . to walk on
earth.

—Thich Nhat Hanh, *The Miracle of Mindfulness*

Our planet is in trouble. Deep trouble. We are destroying
Earth's natural environment at such a rapid rate that it soon
may be unable to sustain us. Widespread pollution, depletion
of resources, human-influenced changes in climate, and
growing overpopulation threaten our very existence as a
species. Experts agree that if dramatic changes in our behavior aren't forthcoming—and soon—Earth's basic ecological
systems could collapse.

What does this have to do with gardening?

Everything.

I'm convinced that gardens—and those who tend them—can help save Earth. Why? Because if we are to survive as a species and preserve the environment on our troubled planet, we must claim, celebrate, and protect our precious bond with nature. We can do this in our gardens. Thankfully, many gardeners already are.

A garden-lover named Gil described his involvement this way: "I have learned to appreciate the wonderful balance of nature, and the fact that there is a balance. Gardening is one of the most kind and useful things that people can do for themselves, and for Earth."

Robert was equally articulate on this subject. "This is a very special time for our planet," he told me. "We hear all manner of ecological messages that say, 'Somebody has to come forward and be accountable. Why not you and me?'

"There's a very close connection between ecological responsibility and gardening, and I feel that's how we're beginning to change human consciousness. Among my fellow gardeners, we're seeing leadership emerge and awareness develop of what this planet is all about. There's a growing sense of our obligation to the generations to come. Social responsibility is emerging from fuller knowledge of just who we are: something we can learn in a garden."

Gil and Robert are on the right track.

I concur with many of my gardening friends who believe that we can find, in even the humblest pot of pansies, something that's missing from the most sophisticated human-built machine: the miracle of nature that not only sustains us, but allows us to feel, to love, and to flourish. If we lose the connection to this wondrous phenomenon, our human race is doomed.

"We cannot make a blade of grass," cultural historian Thomas Berry has pointed out. "Yet, in the future, there's a possibility there isn't going to be so much as a single blade of grass if humans do not protect it, foster it, and in some manner assist in healing the conditions threatening that form of life."

In spite of this sobering prospect, I am hopeful. Notwithstanding Western civilization's near worship of technology and apparent blind faith in "progress" at any price, increasing numbers of my fellow humans join me in being powerfully drawn to the earth, to plants and to the gardens they grow in.

It's no surprise that gardening is the number-one leisure activity in the United States, once you realize how much we seem to need an intimate connection with plants and animals in order to survive. I'm convinced that something precious and vital inside us has atrophied as Western civilization has become more mechanized and less agricultural, more urban and less rural. The garden brings back that bond with the timeless mysteries of nature.

"When nature speaks, we hear the truth of the forces that created us," declared my friend Mark Gerzon, author of *Listening to Midlife,* during an interview at his Colorado home. "If you want to experience this wisdom firsthand, all you have to do is find yourself a garden."

Mark believes, as I do, that there is wisdom that only nature seems to have, that only the natural world is able to teach us. This wisdom is needed to expand and change our consciousness about the environment, a shift that is urgently needed if we are to halt and reverse the ruinous forces humans have unleashed on our planet.

"The image we see in nature's mirror is hard to forget," Mark told me. "It instructs not only our mind but our entire being."

I have had firsthand experience with nature's powerful teachings.

As a teenager in Minnesota, I was fortunate enough to have a girlfriend whose family owned a rustic getaway cabin on an isolated rural lake. One weekend, I was invited to join my friend and her family on an overnight trip to this place. These folks really liked to experience the wildness of the forest. The cabin was shrouded in dense foliage and I remember that we had to hike almost a mile to get to it. When we finally arrived and stowed our gear, I was immersed in a silence so deep and profound that I actually fantasized that I could hear plants growing. One doesn't usually think of teenagers paying attention to any form of silence, but I felt such an intense yet tranquil solitude at this place that I became very quiet inside. The next morning I got up early and went down to the lake, where I sat and listened to a pair of loons piercing the silence in their special way. It was magical.

I learned a real respect for nature during that weekend that has never left me, and I still carry that fathomless silence inside of me. If I'm caught in bumper-to-bumper traffic on a Los Angeles freeway, I find that I can visualize the cabin, the lake, the forest, the loons, and—best of all—the serenity. My heart rate slows down. My breathing deepens. My whole frame of mind changes, and I feel like I'm a thousand miles away. I don't worry about the traffic jam anymore.

When our hearts and souls have been touched by nature in such a fundamental way, I believe we inevitably treat all living things with more respect and concern. We create a garden inside of us that reflects the garden outside of us.

"I've watched many friends as their values change, their goals change, over the years," said my friend Loie, a lifelong gardener. "A great number of these people have become extremely interested in gardening, even if they've barely even glanced at a plant before. I think that connection comes from some place deep within us, some place that is primal."

I asked Loie to describe her own experience of the plant-human bond. I was surprised by her answer.

"Twice in my life I have felt myself 'become one' with the plant I was looking at," she told me. "I'm talking about a complete absorption into the world of plants. You can't make something like this happen through your own free will. It's a kind of transcendental experience that is gone very quickly, but one never forgets it. Becoming one with a plant has fortified my belief that we have a direct relationship to everything that grows, every being that shares energy in this world. I feel a natural connection, as though the energy in the garden is also my energy, as if I'm really part of what's going on. This feeling has made a difference in my entire outlook on life and has prompted me to take an active role in trying to preserve our planet."

I've interviewed many gardeners who, like Loie and me, feel a deep and abiding connection with Earth's marvelously intricate ecology through the experience of working in gardens. Many describe the plot they tend as a "microcosm of a macrocosm"—a world in miniature that contains all the essential components of the whole. Among the world's religious and spiritual traditions, there are many precedents for this holistic way of thinking.

Lama Surya Das, spiritual leader and author of *Awakening the Buddha Within,* noted during one of our conversations that many stories of creation—including the Bible's Garden of Eden—describe gardens as settings of perfection and happiness.

"Gardening gets us back to the source from whence we came," Lama Surya Das emphasized. He described our attraction to gardening as a longing "for a return to nonseparateness, a connecting to Earth and to the primordial purity of things."

A garden, Lama Surya Das speculated, affords us a real experience of life, a chance to think and to act like innocent children again, to celebrate our inborn, childlike sense of awe and wonder.

"By cultivating ourselves in our gardens, we find our origins as human beings. I believe that the phrase 'get back to your roots' is really about returning to this simple but essential state of mind. By connecting externally with the earth, through our gardens, we connect internally as well.

"It's not at all naive to think that gardening can make a difference in terms of saving the planet," said Lama Surya Das when I asked him how important he believed it is for individuals to create gardens. "The Buddha encouraged every monk to plant at least one tree each year. A single tree is worth planting, just as a single thought or action always has some kind of meaning. Every form of life is meant to be cherished, and even one flower or one good deed may go a long way. Who can say one garden or one plant is too small to have value? Collectively, they can have enormous value in terms of their potential to help save our planet from ourselves."

What do you think? Does one garden make a difference?

My answer has been an emphatic "Yes!" ever since I made a trip to Peru several years ago. I journeyed to South America in order to visit the magnificent mountaintop ruins at Machu Picchu. While traveling by bus along the narrow, winding roads of the Andes, I couldn't help but notice that even the tiniest bits of available ground were under some form of cultivation. In this rugged country of grinding poverty, even the steepest hillsides were covered with narrow, terraced plots that grew food for people and their livestock. Yet, I was amazed to see that the gardens closest to the simple adobe homes were overflowing with flowers.

This beautiful bounty surprised me. While those of us who live in the United States tend to buy cut flowers as special treats for ourselves or our loved ones, even the poorest Peruvian families give up a portion of their precious farmland in order to make sure that flowers are an integral part of their daily lives. Everywhere I looked, the otherwise drab landscape was highlighted by bright, colorful flowers. These blossoms seem to be the essence of life for people who otherwise have very little. While desperately trying to fill their stomachs, these farmers were feeding their souls as well.

After my return from Peru, I began to notice how, in my own country, people of every income level and circumstance go to the trouble of creating gardens for themselves. Not far from me, in East Los Angeles, thousands of low-income Mexican and Latin American immigrants maintain minuscule plots of land where corn, beans, squash, and flowers thrive beneath smoggy skies. They are often tucked into tiny wedges of yard or in pots on balconies. As a practical matter, many of these pots and patches don't appear to produce enough food or blossoms to be worth the bother, yet those who tend these flowers and vegetables are passionately devoted to their care.

I believe the nurturing and admiration of even a single plant ties our souls to forces that are vital in nature and that we all long to feel. As symbols of Earth's miraculous gifts, a garden of any size can makes an enormous difference in any life.

Shepherd, the professor turned boysenberry farmer whom you met in the previous chapter, gave me a powerful explanation of gardening's transcendent capacities during our conversation.

"Gardening is one of the best ways to caretake the earth on a small scale," said Shepherd. "There's something about the gardener's various postures—the bowing, kneeling, and getting down on all fours—that shows a strong reverence for the earth. It reminds me that, as the Sufi poet Jelaluddin Rumi said, 'there are hundreds of ways to heal and to kiss the earth,' to honor our spinning green planet."

Shepherd told me that, for him, gardening has a lot of philosophical content functioning from a deep place far beyond his free will.

"Gardening brings me back to the earth—its energies and cycles—in a fundamental and traditional way," he explained. "For instance, I sleep outside as much as I can. It's a different quality of sleep that I get outdoors. I feel a different kind of presence on the earth. I notice things I didn't notice before, like the way the bamboo makes a soft rustling sound in the breeze.

"When I tend my garden, I feel that I am more an integral part of the whole rather than someone distinct from it. Through my gardening, I experience and guide nature directly rather than trying to dominate it or bend it to my will. I only have two acres, but there is so much life here. I have literally hundreds of oaks that are emerging, and I'm protecting them from harm. I feel the life force by letting it be rather than fighting it."

Shepherd said he is fed more by green leaves than by green backs, his satisfactions derive from nature rather than money.

"I like eating something every day that I've grown," he explained. "It makes me feel grounded and connected to the earth. Growing my own food gives me an almost cosmological bond with nature's deep internal rhythm. There is a great deal of mystery, diversity, and fullness to this rhythm. It points beyond the self to the soul and the spirit. There is so much that is always there to sustain us, that is worthy of honoring. For instance, nature has a life-death-and-decay cycle that keeps us going on Earth. We don't fully understand it, but we can see that it exists.

"Much of our world is made up of machines and technology," said Shepherd. "We're surrounded by gadgets, and they don't feed our souls. Our culture is very lost, and we're not in a healthy state as a whole. One way out is by getting back to the earth through gardening. Gardening takes us away from the hyperactivity and chatter of the dominant world. In a garden, we become willing to embrace nature. I go to a special kind of place internally when I'm around my plants. Some of the visitors to my farm start weeping at times because they've really broken their hearts open."

Of course, it's unrealistic to expect that everyone will move to the countryside and plant a big garden, but I agree with Shepherd when he says that there's a lot more available land out there than most people think. Many rural counties in the United States are actually losing population. In contrast, most of our cities are increasingly crowded. Yet even urban and suburban residents can—and do—find a way to connect with their earth through a garden. If they don't have the space or means to cultivate plants of their own, they can always find public gardens and parks in which they can make this connection.

My conversations with people such as Shepherd, Mark, and Lama Surya Das—as well as hundreds of other gardeners—have persuaded me that our culture is struggling to bridge the gap between mind, body, and spirit through the garden. People are seeking new ways to express reverence, celebrate the sacred, and touch the divine. In the garden, many find the connection—and the balance—that they've been craving.

In the Western world, our science and spirituality have

been divorced for much too long. The industrial revolution gave birth to the separation of many things, including the denial of our fundamental human desire for an interactive relationship with nature. Yet everywhere I turn, there is evidence that this wide gap is successfully being bridged.

In her book *Journeying in Place,* author Gunilla Norris provides a wonderful description of her own experience of connecting with nature:

> To gaze into the eye of the ground itself, is it possible? Can the ground be aware of me? This is too strange to speak about, but I do sense the mutuality. This presence upholds my 'creatureliness.' . . . It knows that I breathe and move . . . that I cry and love . . . that I am afraid and exultant . . . that I create and destroy . . . that I hurt and take care. It knows! But not in any way that I can explain.

Over and over, I've noticed that the experience of gardening or having close contact with plants nourishes and nurtures people as nothing else can. People know, instinctively, that time spent in a garden is good for them. How else can one explain the intimate relationship they cultivate with their plants?

"The first thing I do every morning is stand on my second-floor balcony and look at my garden," Rebecca told me. "Then I come downstairs, have a cup of coffee, and stare out at the garden again. I don't care if there's only one new bloom, it just feels so delightful to stand and look. That's pure joy. It makes me feel better about myself, as if I'm feeding my soul.

"I've been dating this absolutely wonderful man," Rebecca continued. "He's the most sensitive guy I've ever known and yet he doesn't know one flower from the next. In fact, I don't think he ever noticed flowers before he met me.

"Well, one weekend we were visiting some rural property he owns in Wisconsin, and I suddenly called out to him, 'Come here, Bill. You've simply got to see this!' I showed him some lovely orange wildflowers mixed in with the trillium, where I had found the most marvelous little orange-and-brown butterfly sitting among the blossoms. After looking at this in silence, Bill turned to me and whispered, 'Becky, I've never noticed anything like that before.'

"Since then, Bill's gotten more in touch with nature and it's amazing to see the little things that he notices now. It's such a joy. I guess that's what I would like to leave as my legacy, a gift of having enabled people to enjoy nature, to feed their souls, and to help them save our planet."

When I talk with my fellow gardeners, I am heartened to discover the depth of love they feel for our beleaguered Earth. Like me, they are head over heels in love with the beauty of the natural world. Yet many of them are fearful of what looms ahead. They have read dire news reports about the escalating rate of extinction among plant and animal species in every type of environment. They worry about the ongoing destruction of the rain forest and of the stands of timber within our borders. They know that we are rapidly depleting our finite supplies of coal, oil, and natural gas and that our pollutants are fouling the air, land, oceans, and rivers. Everywhere they turn, the predictions are grim.

The dimensions of what's happening seem to be of an order of magnitude far beyond what Earth has previously experienced. In sharing these fears, I can't help but wonder why humans—who have supposedly created the most advanced civilizations that have ever been—seem so bent on destroying the ecological web that allows our community of life to exist. The stability of these fragile systems seems to rest in the diversity of their many parts. Yet we are destroying these components day by day, little by little.

No one will ever see a living Carolina parakeet or a passenger pigeon, yet in nineteenth-century America, there were millions of these birds. Nor will we ever know with any precision the true value of such extinct species in the natural order of things. As our lives become more separated from nature's great diversity, our direct knowledge and experience of these losses dims.

"We are living in a very sterile, artificial world, almost totally removed from nature," my gardening friend Anna pointed out. "As I walk through big cities, I see the concrete-and-steel environment that people are cooped up in all day long. Plants put us back in touch with the natural world that we come from. Even if it's unconscious, people feel a need for more than paper, computers, and TV. Something as simple as walking into a nursery or garden center can help meet that need within us.

"I can see how my own relationship to plants transforms me," Anna continued. "Plants help me grow stronger. They turn my world into a wonderful, magical, and beautiful place.

I've discovered that nature can change me unlike anything else. The garden brings me the essence of peace, the full meaning of being alone and of being quiet. I'm absolutely certain that there's some kind of 'soul connection' between humans and plants. It's something that happens on a nonverbal level, not on an intellectual one."

The feelings Anna talked about lie just below the surface in nearly all of the conversations I've had with other gardeners. These folks talk about having "a hunger"—sometimes even "a great craving"—to bond with nature. A part of their being simply cries out to be in a garden or a park.

The human urge to experience nature is something that the most sensitive city planners and architects know about. This explains, in part, why islands of greenery attract so many city dwellers who are eager to relax and enjoy themselves among plants. Even corporations are creating miniature parks and landscaped courtyards at places where people work, a confirmation of both the therapeutic and aesthetic value of gardens. It is through this rapport and harmony that we absorb the wisdom of Earth—and find ourselves strengthened from the connection. We ignore this essential component in modern life at our peril.

William Logan, author of *Dirt: The Ecstatic Skin of the Earth*, believes that digging and puttering around in a garden puts us in direct contact with the laws by which our planet exists, and by which all of its life forms subsist. Through this communion, we can become entranced and rejuvenated by the divine presence in nature.

"Gardening is a unique collaboration," Logan told me,

"because we're asking Mother Nature to bring forth something in particular—and that won't happen without a great deal of mutual understanding and awareness. It is not often in our lives that we get a chance to participate in such a direct way with helping the processes of nature. Yet when we do, we are energized."

Logan confirmed the mind-boggling statistics I'd read about the destruction humans are wreaking on their planet. By the late 1990s, we were destroying over seventy-five billion tons of topsoil each year, along with trillions of gallons of natural gas and oil. The very foundation of modern Western civilization rests on these basic resources, yet neither topsoil nor petroleum can be replaced by nature within the foreseeable future.

"We humans, as a species, have really taken over Earth during the twentieth century," Logan told me. "In places where farming has been mechanized, the effects on the topsoil are pretty disastrous. At the rate we're using up these soils, they simply will not be around much longer. Even in Hawaii, one of the most fertile places on the entire planet, it takes two thousand years for nature to create an inch of new topsoil. Can we ever hope to recover from such devastation?"

I asked Logan if, as an expert on the important role soil plays in our environment, he ever felt frustrated in his attempts to call attention to the disaster that overshadows our future. The frustration is not so much in cultivating awareness of the problem, said Logan, but in motivating individuals to modify their conduct or to take direct action.

"There's a crazy discontinuity between what people know

in their hearts to be true and what they actually do in their day-to-day behavior," said Logan. "We live in a time when the difference between those two realities is sometimes excruciatingly painful."

Another important thinker who has commented on this "crazy discontinuity" is cultural historian, former priest, and author Thomas Berry, founder of New York's Riverdale Center for Religious Studies. The crux of the environmental crisis, according to Berry, lies in the fact that the underlying structure of Western life is based on the notion that all inherent rights and values belong to the humans, while the non-human world is relegated to "being used" by them.

"Everything has rights, and all living things are needed," said Berry in an audio-published interview with Brian Swimme, director of the Center for the Story of the Universe. "Humans have their value, flowers have their value, but the real value lies in the total community."

In short, all living things are necessary for the survival of everything else, and we have no right to exploit them in a thoughtless, limitless way. Yet each of the Western world's major social institutions—religion, government, the law, media, education, and business—is doing little or nothing to curb such unlimited exploitation and abuse. Indeed, in many instances they are encouraging it.

"They are not guiding us," Berry complained of our institutions and leaders. "They have not shown how we should deal with our presence on the planet, of how humans should relate to the other-than-human world, the more-than-human world."

Yet a few cracks are appearing in the armor that shields these powerful forces from the warnings of whistle-blowers like Thomas Berry and William Logan. The cracks are being made—and widened—by the millions of gardeners who make a soulful connection with our "more-than-human world" through the tending of their plants. In increasing numbers, these gardeners also happen to be individuals with direct access to the levers of institutional power and influence. Take Mark Gerzon, for instance.

A colleague of mine for several years, Mark has long nurtured and explored his fascination with the intersection of body, mind, and spirit. It is here, in the ill-defined confluence of conscious and unconscious intelligence, that my friend explores new concepts of reality, innovative interpretations of our past, and exciting possibilities for our collective future.

A humanitarian social activist as well as a teacher and author, Mark has worked closely with politicians and entertainment industry executives in fashioning a more heart centered approach to government, mass media, and business. During the early 1990s, Mark midwifed a dialogue between media figures in Hollywood and the Soviet Union with the goal of increasing understanding between these two very different cultures. A few years later, he set up consciousness-raising sessions with half the members of Congress that were designed to bring a more holistic approach to legislative problem solving. It was toward the end of the latter project that Mark had an experience in nature that changed his life.

"The uncertainty, anxiety, and pressure of dealing with people on Capitol Hill had really gotten to me, and I started having an intolerable chest pain," recalled Mark. "The various relaxation tricks I'd learned—meditation, exercise, deep breathing, resting, massage—didn't help. I tried them all and nothing got rid of this terrible pain. Sometimes it would keep me awake all night, other times it would wake me up at four in the morning. It was a classic physical symptom of stress.

"One day I took a walk in the mountains and totally submerged myself in nature. Something in the trees, flowers, and wildlife around me silently spoke to me. I realized that I simply had to give up and ask for help. I wanted guidance from the life force that I felt all around me.

"For the first time I can remember, I began to pray out loud. I was looking at the mountains and the sky as I was praying, addressing myself to 'the creator of life'—or what other people might call 'God.'

"I said, 'I can't do this by myself. I took this job with Congress in order to do God's will, and it's only fair that God be with me at this moment.' I prayed and cried for at least a half hour. When I was done I felt that I had opened up a relationship with the divine that I'd never had before.

"When I look back at that encounter, I realize that it was a classic spiritual experience. I know that they tend to come when we're unhappy and at the end of our tether, when we're finally ready to surrender and willing to ask for help. All of the great and creative spiritual leaders have had experiences like this, of realizing that they need assistance from something larger than themselves.

"The pain in my chest gradually went away. Sometimes it comes back in a much milder form, almost like a knock on the door. Now I translate it into meaning, 'There is someone or something that you're not paying attention to right now, and you really need to.' I know that this is my higher self—or God—reminding me that I'm losing my way. These pains are like alarm bells that wake me up."

Mark Gerzon now believes—and I wholeheartedly agree with him—that nature is sounding alarm bells linked to its own survival. They represent a wake-up call for the human race, an urgent plea for us to take quick action in defense of Earth. Mark is now speaking out—through his books, workshops, and lectures—on the need for us to persuade our institutions and leaders to assert such action. His is one of a gathering chorus of influential voices that is making a positive difference. The message is clear: We need to assume responsibility not simply for our own behavior but for the behavior of the human race as a whole. We are all in this together.

"If the planet does not function, we are not going to function," Thomas Berry has warned. You cannot have well humans on a sick planet. . . . Our solution lies in the rediscovery of our integral connection with Earth."

The essential content of what Berry says is not new. What's changed is the urgency of the message. It's been two centuries since Thomas Jefferson—the third United States president and a proud farmer—wrote the following:

> The Earth belongs to the living, and no man can by natural right oblige the land he occupies, or the persons that succeed him in that occupation, to the debts contracted by him. For if he could, he might

during his own life eat up the use of the lands for several generations to come. Then the Earth would belong to the dead and not to the living generation.

The fact that Jefferson's pro-environment message has not been heeded is a solemn reminder that it's not enough for our foremost thinkers and most powerful politicians to act and advocate on behalf of nature. The rest of us must get involved too. We must act on our belief that Earth is worth saving. I am happy to report that this is already the case among a growing percentage of the gardeners—and garden-admirers—with whom I speak.

Here are some excerpts from my conversations:

"I think gardening is biological," said Diane. "I think it's something that humans were meant to do. When I wonder about how we can solve juvenile crime, I can only conclude that we've got to get these kids back into the garden. I spend part of every day in my garden, and it has more positive benefits for me than I can tell you."

Sue declared that "the activity of gardening is the most positive thing that anyone can be involved in. You start out with a tiny seed and you get a flower. You're outside. You're exercising. You're at peace. You're healing the planet. It's totally satisfying."

"Wisdom comes with years," Loie mused, "and it isn't the same as when you started gardening. At this stage in my gardening life, I'm trying to think like Buddha. I sit and cultivate the silence now. I've stopped worrying about things that aren't getting done, and I'm trying to live in the present moment. I do the rest of it when I'm in the mood."

"Gardening is like meditation for me," declared Bonnie, "a way for me to express the sense of honor that I have for this earth and the way that it nurtures me. I am enriched by the beauty of my plants. They tend my soul."

"I love to put flowers that I've grown into vases," Martha told me. "I love to have a table on which there's [a meal] made from the food I grow. It makes me feel self-sufficient and abundant and strong. These are all illusions, of course. I live in a city. I buy seeds. I'm not some kind of earth goddess. But it makes me feel that, for perhaps ten minutes at a time, I can be the earth goddess."

"There's something very primal about a garden," said Sonja, a New Yorker interviewed during a lunch-hour visit to one of Manhattan's many public gardens. "I believe that the wisest people are reincarnated as gardeners. They seem to be the planet's oldest souls, the ones most connected to the earth."

One of my favorite stories was related to me by Barbara, and concerned her cat, Max: "In his youth, Max killed a bullfrog and left the poor thing under my apple tree, where I eventually found it. I decided to leave the body there, believing that it would add something to the earth and maybe make the apples taste better. About two weeks later I noticed that a mushroom of some kind had exploded through the belly of the dead animal. The spores obviously had been in the ground beneath the apple tree, and now this new living thing was thriving on the decomposed body of the bullfrog. That scene was such a wonderful metaphor for the life cycles of nature that I went out and took a picture of it. I've never thought about my garden in the same way since I witnessed this extraordinary event.'"

Actor Eddie Albert, star of the 1960s hit TV series *Green Acres,* is another lifelong gardener who has been deeply touched by his experiences with plants. Since the early 1970s, he's helped establish hundreds of inner-city community gardens. He has warned about topsoil erosion since the Great Depression, when he was deeply shocked to see New York City enveloped in a dust cloud that resulted from land abuse. Albert loves to grow organic corn, beans, and melons in his frontyard, using earth-friendly methods handed down from Native Americans.

During one of our many conversations, Albert recalled an incident involving his son, who was six years old at the time. Young Edward pushed a series of brass tacks into the trunk of an enormous backyard tree, spelling out his initials.

"My wife and I thought it was fun to look at, but we really didn't give it much thought," Eddie recalled. "But about five years later, the same tree began a noticeable decline. This tree was well over one hundred years old, mind you, and very solid. Our son could climb up into that tree and you couldn't see him—that's how big and serious a tree it was.

"The tree was obviously sick and I had so-called experts come in and take a look. None of them could tell me what was wrong. It was so devastating to watch this marvelous thing die. I tried every possible remedy, to no avail. It was our best tree, our favorite tree.

"At one point during this period I was in Indochina, walking with a fellow in a rubber plantation. In the course of our discussion, the man told me that the Japanese, on their World War II march to Singapore, had killed the first growth of rubber trees on this plantation by pounding a copper nail into each trunk. The soldiers knew that one small nail could end a tree's life.

"There was a kind of hush as I asked myself, *When is the next airplane back to Los Angeles?*

"So I came back and immediately ran to our dying tree and pulled out all of those little brass tacks. The tree stopped deteriorating and, little by little, it got its strength back. Now I'm convinced that it's going to keep on going for another hundred years.

"This incident taught me how closely we are linked to the plants we tend, how interdependent our relationship is. And you know something? I have never taken a tree—or any other plant—for granted since the day I yanked those tacks out."

Stories like these are compelling testimonials to the power of gardens to change attitudes, as well as behavior. All it takes is a single incident to alter our awareness and lifestyles forever.

At this point, you may be wondering how any one person can really make a difference in halting the juggernaut of environmental destruction that threatens Earth. After all, if powerful people like Thomas Jefferson, Al Gore, astronomer Carl Sagan, and *Silent Spring* author Rachel Carson have been unable to put a dent in the status quo, then how can we expect to effect any meaningful change?

The fact is, we can. And we do. Little by little, step by step, each of makes a difference in the overall health of our planet. The simple act of cultivating can enrich the soil, pump oxygen into the air, and provide habitat for wildlife, while providing food, shade, and serenity for the gardener. Beyond that, of course, is the potential for a change in awareness that can affect many aspects of our attitudes and behavior.

One of the most inspiring stories I've read about shifts in consciousness involves former United States Foreign Service officer John Graham, as printed in the anthology entitled *Earth and Spirit: The Spiritual Dimension of the Environmental Crisis.*

Graham spent his early professional life as a political military officer, advising third world governments on how to control uprisings and dissent. Until his midthirties, he was "helping fuel endless cycles of mindless violence" in war-torn places like Vietnam. Although he later did a more humanitarian type of diplomacy work in Africa and at the United Nations, Graham was too scared to make the important changes in his life that he intuitively knew were necessary.

The "major shove" that Graham needed came in the form of a 1980 cruise-ship disaster in the Gulf of Alaska that saw him, an onboard lecturer, thrown into storm-tossed seas that threatened to swamp the lifeboat he shared with seven other passengers. A howling gale and thirty-foot waves made it impossible for rescue helicopters to fly, and Graham was sure he and his companions would die of exposure or drowning.

Death was staring him in the face. At first Graham was angry that, just as he was starting to do "good work" in his profession, his life was going to end. Graham began a dialogue in his mind with God, protesting what seemed an unfair turn of events. Then, out of the storm, a very clear, strong voice seemed to speak to him. It was as though the truth of his unconscious was manifesting itself.

"That voice said that I was still playing life as if it were a game; that I was eager to talk about my ideals, but still not serious about putting them into action," Graham later wrote. "If I was going to continue to misuse my talents, the voice continued, I might as well end my life out in the storm. But if I was willing to get serious about pursuing my true life's work . . . well, the choice was mine."

John Graham got serious. In the instant he made the decision to wholeheartedly direct his talents toward serving humanity, a Coast Guard cutter emerged from the tempest and rescued all the passengers aboard Graham's lifeboat.

After returning to New York, Graham began leading workshops and lecturing on the subject of peaceful political change. He became a collaborator with many of the individuals and groups he'd previously been working against. Two years later, Graham got involved in the Giraffe Project, a nonprofit organization that finds, honors, and publicizes people who are "sticking their necks out for the common good." Many of these "giraffes" are working hard, against all odds, to improve the natural environment on Mother Earth. Through Graham's efforts, our planet is a better place. Yet he would be the first to concede that much more needs to be done.

"What's most lacking," according to Graham, "is public-spirited courage. . . . A lack of brains or good intentions is not the problem. We need more people with ideas and ideals who are sticking their necks out to put those ideas and ideals into action."

When we accept our share of responsibility for today's environmental crisis—and do something to try to solve it—positive change inevitably will occur. In Graham's view, it's not just adults who need to take up this challenge: young people do too. Cultivating a commitment to service and responsible citizenship among children and teenagers must be a high priority.

"Schools need to teach that the nonhuman world has rights that humans are morally and legally bound to respect," environmental writer Thomas Berry has suggested. "Every being has at least three rights: the right to exist, the right to habitat, and the right to fulfill its role in the ever-renewing process of nature."

During the course of my research for this book, I've deliberately sought out individuals who are sharing their gardening expertise and environmental concern with young people. I greatly admire the way they are able to convey an experience of the wonders and preciousness of the natural world. It is through their efforts, I believe, that the wisdom of gardening can best be passed along to the next generation, who will likely face an even more daunting task than my generation does in preserving our planet.

"We all came from this earth and we're all going to go back to it," said James, an environmental educator working with children in a large public garden complex. "Everything that comes from the earth eventually returns to the earth. So why not try to take care of it?

"The most damaging animal is the human being," James continued. "People need to understand that by working together we can extend the life on this planet, because human beings will perish if we don't. I teach children gardening because they are going to have to take over from us and keep this planet going. If we don't teach them about tending Earth, this important information is going to be lost. We have city kids who see nothing but a supermarket when they get their food. They enjoy it, but they have no idea where what they eat comes from. All adults have a responsibility to tell young people how this food comes to be on this earth. It doesn't just happen, the miracles of nature have to create food.

"I explain to children that when we get thirsty, we want a drink of water. I tell them that a plant in a garden, when it gets thirsty, will wither because it cannot ask for a drink of water. When you get cold, you want to put on a sweater. The plant can't put on a sweater. If the plant can't survive the cold, you must bring it to where it can keep warm. If you can't get food, water, and warmth, you will die. A plant is no different."

Anna is also an environmental educator, a colleague of James.

"If we're not teaching our young people the value of natural habitats such as wetlands," she said, "then they grow up being indifferent to the protection of these habitats. Children, obviously, are our future. This is why gardening with kids is so important.

"As more of our land is developed, it becomes absolutely crucial that we set aside more space for parks and for gardens," Anna continued. "Did you know that we've already lost 75 percent of our wetlands in the United States? Many were destroyed because we didn't understand their value. As a result, we have a lot more flooding, because we don't have any place for excess water to go when there are downpours.

I'm not even mentioning the value of the lost plants and animals, like ducks and frogs."

Larry also teaches children about the environment for a living. His grandparents were farmers, and Larry is passing on much of the appreciation for nature that he learned from them.

"One thing the kids and I do is create 'peace gardens,'" Larry told me, "by using plants that are native to countries throughout the world. I tell stories that reflect on what is special about each of these countries, with a focus on the environment. In this way, we sensitize children to nature and to conservation issues as well as encourage an appreciation of other cultures.

"The garden is a great learning tool," he continued. "For example, I asked one boy to help me with the compost pile. As we were mixing in the table scraps and dirt and manure, I told him we were making a sort of Disneyland for worms. I explained that while this material might be pretty disgusting to us, worms like nothing better. So this boy went around for the rest of the day excitedly telling people that he'd spent the morning creating a worm Disneyland. He was terrific.

"Another time, I told my kids we had to pull weeds from our garden or else it would suck the life out of our flowers and vegetables. They decided that the weeds were like vampires and created a name for themselves: weed terminators. They spent all afternoon eagerly going about a task that most people can't stand. They made weeding fun for themselves, which is a great way to get kids hooked on gardening—and on saving the environment."

At a luxuriant public garden in Harlem, I talked to Haja,

whose children—and neighbors' children—had helped turn a trash-strewn vacant lot into a verdant urban oasis.

"What goes on here goes way beyond gardening," Haja insisted. "It all started because we were dissatisfied with looking out and seeing garbage piled up. We thought, *Why not get the whole neighborhood involved in cleaning the place up?* So that's exactly what we did.

"As far as I'm concerned," he continued, "there's no end to what you can accomplish once you get something like this going. We've gotten a lot of kids and teenagers involved in getting the garden organized. They help us put up fences and move dirt and so on. Without the garden, a lot of them probably would have been off somewhere getting into trouble."

Creating and tending a garden shows young people that there's something beyond what's immediately in front of them, both literally and figuratively. It can teach them more about the world, about attaining an overarching balance and perspective in their lives. They learn patience, social skills, and the necessity of working hard for things they really want.

"My life has changed immeasurably as a result of this garden," Haja said. "At first, I wondered if it made sense to keep working in the garden, when people threw garbage over the fence and broke the trees and stole garden tools. It was really frustrating. I asked myself, *Is it worth it?* But over the last ten years, things have really changed for the better. Now there are a lot of people who defend the garden, who've made it an extension of their lives."

In his profession as an ordained minister, Haja believes

gardening has helped him become a good steward of the earth, no longer taking it for granted.

"A garden helps you put your signature on the ground in a productive way," he concluded. "It stimulates me to grow as a person, to cultivate and renew myself, to fill myself up so that I can give to others again. In a sense, we have home-steaded the land. It takes a different mentality, a different frame of reference, to see the value of our beautiful garden versus a plot of ugly, raw land waiting to be developed in the middle of a New York City slum."

There are as many ways to honor, celebrate, and heal the earth as there are people. The same holds true for environ-mental education. The kind of apprenticeship carried out in urban gardens is an effective approach, yet young people—and adults—can just as easily acquire the wisdom of garden-ing through less formal encounters. Walk down the street and smell the flowers, go on a vacation and tour a national park, talk to your neighbor about the threats to our planet: an opportunity to learn and teach awaits you.

Examples abound.

Florida gardener and artist Nancy Forrester, whom you met in the preceding chapter, encourages visitors of all ages to tour the last vestige of green earth in downtown Key West, Florida. For more than thirty years, her commitment to Nancy's Secret Garden has been unwavering.

"Folks who come here to visit my little jungle are part of a wave of garden-lovers that will only be getting bigger and big-ger in years to come," Nancy predicted. "These are lovely and loving people who have begun to fully appreciate the earth and the role of nature in our lives. School children come by the busload now and are especially appreciative. I give all of them guided tours of my garden, and I can tell that sometimes it completely changes their lives.

"This sort of work is a tremendous responsibility," stressed Nancy, acknowledging that few among us are up to the task of creating a miniature rain forest. "The garden grew out of my deciding early on that I would choose art and quality human interactions as the core of my life. What I have created is a sanctuary. I've learned kind of a universal knowledge from my plants. I have tried desperately to save them, and I'm passing all that along to the next generation."

I applaud Nancy and the thousands of other dedicated and selfless gardeners who are working so hard to make our planet a better place—and to share the miracles of nature. Their efforts remind me of something that Kentucky farmer and author Wendell Berry once wrote: "The world cannot be discovered by a journey of miles, however long, but only by a spiritual journey, a journey of one inch very arduous and humble and joyful, by which we arrive at the ground at our feet, and learn to be at home."

How then, knowing all this, shall we live?

I don't have specific answers, yet I am convinced that we need to make far-reaching and dramatic changes in our lives if we are to readjust our relationship with Earth in a way that assures the planet's survival. Most important, we are going to have to recover our appreciation of nature and of the sacred and spiritual wisdom that comes to us through our natural environment. In order to accomplish these goals, many of our institutions will also have to change, including our economic systems, courts, schools, religions, and governments. I do not pretend to be an expert on how this should be accomplished. In fact, I believe it will take all of our collective psychic and intellectual energy to figure out the best ways to implement such changes. As Thomas Berry puts it, a shift in environmental consciousness is "the historical mission of our times," one that calls to the deepest capacity of the human soul.

According to Berry, "in the twentieth century the glory of the human has become the desolation of Earth, and this desolation is becoming the destiny of all humans. All of our institutions and activities must now be judged primarily to the extent to which they inhibit, ignore, or foster a mutually enhancing human/Earth relationship."

I am not a Pollyanna. It would be naive to believe that the major changes we must make will not affect the affluent lifestyles that most of us in highly industrialized nations currently enjoy. There will be dislocation and discomfort as we reduce our horrendous rates of consumption, waste, and misuse. We will have to give up certain privileges and perks that we've come to regard as inalienable rights. For example, we may need to cut back on our use of gasoline, water, forest products, and electricity in order to conserve these resources for future generations. There is also a risk that even these kinds of changes won't be enough and that more draconian measures will be needed. Yet if we don't accept such disruptions and realignments in our daily lives, the environmental crisis can only get worse in the long run.

We live in a rare moment of grace, an era during which the potential for transformation of our awareness is suspended in the air—and our future hangs in the balance. Writer Donald Peakie reminds us that "nothing in this world is really precious until we know that it will soon be gone."

This is an exciting and challenging time to be alive, in spite of all the pessimistic prophecies and discouraging news about the environment. In times of trauma and disaster, individuals throughout history have acted heroically. It is a tribute to the human spirit that, historically, there are always at least a few among us who rise to the occasion and take appropriate action for the common good. I believe they will do so again, and I urge all of us to join hands in supporting their efforts.

Rather than shrink from the formidable tasks that face the human race, I'm hopeful that we may soon celebrate and embrace these challenges with the best that our brains, bodies, and hearts have to offer. Many experts are already rising to the challenge. Pioneers in biointensive gardening, for instance, say they have developed new forms of pesticide-free, soil-building farming that could feed all of the world's people in the twenty-first century. And in the field of alternative energy, scientists have made great strides in developing affordable electricity from such renewable resources as the sun, wind, and water.

As each of us develops an expanded awareness of our environmental problems, a shift in our consciousness as a species could very well bring us the answers—and action—we are seeking. If all of us are motivated by our passionate hearts to change, if we allow our dreams of a better future to drive our actions, we can heal our collective soul, our civilization, and our planet at the same time. I am convinced that this will ultimately curtail the destructive activities that imperil us, and make the world a better place than we have ever imagined it could become.

I leave you with one last bit of wisdom that has fueled my optimism since the day I encountered it. At the end of a July 1998 conference of the Noetic Sciences Society, the group's founder—former astronaut Edgar Mitchell, the sixth man to walk on the moon—quoted the following Sanskrit saying:

> God sleeps in the minerals
> Awakens in the plants
> Walks in the animals
> And thinks in man.

For me, this passage says it all. On the spinning, blue-green orb we call Earth, the welfare of even the smallest plant or animal is inextricably linked to the well-being of all others. The task of preserving that web of life is potentially the biggest challenge ever posed to the beings who think—the beings called human. Yet successfully meeting that challenge could bring us the most satisfying rewards that any civilization has never known. I am exceedingly hopeful that it will.

Maybe—just maybe—gardening can help save Earth. It can unquestionably help us protect our souls from the potential sterility of an increasingly technological society and allow us to reconnect with the creative magic of the natural world. Whether we're admiring roses in a neighbor's garden, eating tomatoes from our backyard vegetable patch, or enjoying the shady splendor of a city park, we can each still nurture our own small reminder of our responsibility in creating and preserving our Earth—our celestial Eden.

## About the Authors

Connie Goldman is an author, speaker, independent public radio producer, and former staff member of National Public Radio in Washington, D.C. She is the coauthor, with Richard Mahler, of *Secrets of Becoming a Late Bloomer: Extraordinary Ordinary People on the Art of Staying Creative, Alive, and Aware in Midlife and Beyond* and coauthor, with Phillip Berman, of *The Ageless Spirit.* Based in Santa Monica, California, Goldman's nonprofit production company develops radio programming and audiocassettes that offer insight, inspiration, and motivation for personal growth in midlife and beyond. For information, visit her Web site at www.congoldman.org or write to Connie Goldman Productions, 926 Second Street, Suite 201, Santa Monica, California 90403.

Richard Mahler is an award-winning author, journalist, and radio producer who has written extensively about the environment, personal growth, travel, and the arts. Mahler coauthored, with Connie Goldman, *Secrets of Becoming a Late Bloomer: Extraordinary Ordinary People on the Art of Staying Creative, Alive, and Aware in Midlife and Beyond.* Based in Santa Fe, New Mexico, he has taught classes and workshops on meditation, writing, and storytelling. Mahler welcomes comments and inquiries sent in care of Hazelden, P.O. Box 176, Center City, Minnesota 55012-0176.

**Hazelden Information and Educational Services** is a division of the Hazelden Foundation, a not-for-profit organization. Since 1949, Hazelden has been a leader in promoting the dignity and treatment of people afflicted with the disease of chemical dependency.

The mission of the foundation is to improve the quality of life for individuals, families, and communities by providing a national continuum of information, education, and recovery services that are widely accessible; to advance the field through research and training; and to improve our quality and effectiveness through continuous improvement and innovation.

Stemming from that, the mission of this division is to provide quality information and support to people wherever they may be in their personal journey—from education and early intervention, through treatment and recovery, to personal and spiritual growth.

Although our treatment programs do not necessarily use everything Hazelden publishes, our bibliotherapeutic materials support our mission and the Twelve Step philosophy upon which it is based. We encourage your comments and feedback.

The headquarters of the Hazelden Foundation is in Center City, Minnesota. Additional treatment facilities are located in Chicago, Illinois; New York, New York; Plymouth, Minnesota; St. Paul, Minnesota; and West Palm Beach, Florida. At these sites, we provide a continuum of care for men and women of all ages. Our Plymouth facility is designed specifically for youth and families.

For more information on Hazelden, please call 1-800-257-7800. Or you may access our World Wide Web site on the Internet at **www.hazelden.org**.